We are Beth-El Nurses:
A Heritage of Caring
at the
Foot of Pikes Peak

JOANNE F. RUTH

To Jamie,

Caring is our Gift
to the Future.

Jo Ruth

10-26-16

Happy 65th
Birthday
Live Long!

DEDICATION

To all the nurses of Beth-El—the dedicated caregivers who have come before, those who currently care for all in need, and those yet to come. This is for you.

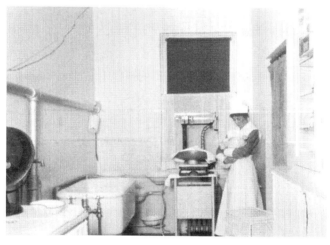

(For photo reference of nurses' portrait on front cover, see page 73.)

ACKNOWLEDGEMENTS

The history of Beth-El College of Nursing belongs to and comes to us through the individual hearts, minds, and actions of hundreds of alumni. Individuals from our various schools of nursing, hospitals, educational institutions, and Methodist organizations have dug deep into their memories and archives to share thoughts, questions, and validation. Individuals and organizations in our community and state have eagerly contributed important insight into the value and depth of the impact that Beth-El nurses have had and continue to have on the health of the citizens of Colorado Springs.

Thank you to the many individuals who have offered encouragement, documentation of information, and valuable critique through the years. Tim Blevins and Mary Davis of The Pikes Peak Library District, Special Collection, have been uniquely instrumental in bringing this story to life. Family and friends have listened and offered encouragement during the long process of collecting the proud story of Beth-El nurses.

Image Acknowledgements

Throughout the years, individual Beth-El alumni of the Beth-El Hospital and the School of Nursing have contributed many of the images presented in this book to the Beth-El Alumni Archives. The names of individual donors of the images are identified if known.

Images: Courtesy of Pikes Peak Library District
          Courtesy of UCCS Archives Kraemer Family Library, University of Colorado Colorado Springs.

TABLE OF CONTENTS

Dear Readers:

It has been with the greatest care and effort that I have striven to recognize and name each individual whose picture appears in "We Are Beth-El Nurses," but some I have been unable to identify. The possibility exists, too, that I may have misidentified someone, considering the years that have passed, the subjective input from a multitude of people who have generously offered their memories, or just simply human error. For any mistakes, I apologize and take responsibility. And at the same time, I whole-heartedly invite you, my readers, to share any corrections with me that you may have. Please contact me if you know any unidentified persons, corrected dates, or if you believe a face matched with a name is in error.

In addition, I would like to invite any of you with stories of your own about Beth-El, our nurses, or our history to share your memories with me. I want to hear what you remember, and if you'll allow me, to share those stories with others, either via Facebook or subsequent editions of "We Are Beth-El Nurses."

In grateful anticipation,
Jo Ruth
Bethel.nurses@gmail.com
www.facebook.com/BethElNurses

PREFACE

We are Beth-El Nurses: A Heritage of Caring at the Foot of Pikes Peak is the affirmative response to the question "Nurse…Nurse…Do We Have a Nurse?"

In June of 2008, I originally presented "Nurse…Nurse…Do We Have a Nurse?," as a brief history of Beth-El College of Nursing and Health Sciences University of Colorado at Colorado Springs (UCCS), at the Pikes Peak Regional History Symposium: Doctors, Disease and Dying in the Pikes Peak Region.

We are Beth-El Nurses: A Heritage of Caring at the Foot of Pikes Peak is the basis for a chapter entitled "Nurse…Nurse…Do We Have a Nurse," written for publication in the Pikes Peak Library District Eleventh Annual History Symposium publication *Bigwigs & Benefactors of the Pikes Peak Region,* scheduled for a 2016 release. This book expands and deepens the presentation of the evolving progress of a Colorado Springs nursing school. The school, originally named Deaconess Training School, became Beth-El Training School, then **Beth-El School of Nursing**, and eventually transitioned to **Beth-El College of Nursing and Health Sciences of the University of Colorado at Colorado Springs** (the "at" was dropped by the university in 2011 as required by the U.S. post office). Through the dedication of the alumni, who have treasured their individual memories of the 110-year story of Beth-El School of Nursing, I am returning this improbable success story to you, the people of the Pikes Peak region. The citizens of Colorado are the benefactors, as well as beneficiaries of the continuity of care provided by dedicated Beth-El Nurses.

In 2015, the CU Board of Regents voted unanimously to name the college the Helen and Arthur E. Johnson Beth-El College of Nursing and Health Sciences in recognition of the $8 million endowment gift received from the Denver-based Helen and Arthur E. Johnson Foundation. Lynn Champion, chairman of the Foundation affirmed, "The Beth-El College of Nursing is an outstanding program and its efforts are imperative to address the nursing shortage in our state, especially in rural Colorado."[1]

The alumni truly are coauthors as they share memories and perspectives of nursing care and educational experiences. Julia Ray Work, a 1913 graduate, along with Margaret Glew, a 1912 graduate, wrote a small, vibrant history of the "early days" at Deaconess Hospital. The Colorado Conference of Woman's Home Missionary Society (WHMS) of the Methodist Episcopal Church located in Denver was instrumental in the founding of our first hospital and training school, which they named "Colorado Conference Deaconess Hospital." Students and local citizens sometimes informally referred to the hospital as "Old Deaconess."

Marjorie Henderson Martin, a 1927 graduate, led the alumnae in creating four large scrapbooks of valuable images and Beth-El history during the 1960s and 1970s. Mrs. Ollie J. Smith, secretary of the local Board of Managers for Deaconess Hospital and Beth-El Hospital and Women's Board of Beth-El Hospital, faithfully recorded the minutes from 1904 to 1943. Her summary notes of the founding, and their continued faithful support of the hospital and training school, offer a unique first-person account of the dedication and ongoing struggle to provide care for citizens of the Pikes Peak region and Colorado.

Cheri Robinson Gillard, class of 1984, Beth-El School of Nursing, combined her unique knowledge of publishing and nursing in the preparation of the manuscript into this book that you hold in your hands.

The Pikes Peak region became an emotional home for me and my family when I was a child. We returned yearly for refreshing respites from the hot, incessant summer winds of western Kansas. Since 1970, I have been "at home" in Colorado Springs, most of that time associated with Beth-El School or College of Nursing. As a faculty member, I had the privilege of meeting alumnae and eagerly listening to the "Beth-El history" they exchanged with each other. The alumnae returned their intimate knowledge of the history of the school, which unfortunately had been almost lost to current students and faculty, as well as to the staff of Memorial Hospital, and citizens of Colorado Springs. We celebrated our eightieth anniversary in 1984. In recognition of my role in reviving knowledge of the Beth-El School of Nursing, I received an honorary diploma from Beth-El School of Nursing at the 1984 graduation at the Alumni's request.

I remain deeply honored to be an adopted "Beth-El Nurse," historian, and active member of the Beth-El Alumni.

Jo Ruth

---

[1] Lynn Campion, Chairman, Helen and Arthur E. Johnson, in UCCS Press release, Colorado Springs, April 20, 2015, 2.

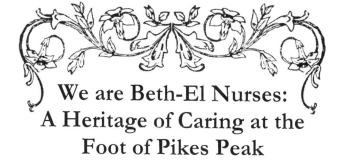

We are Beth-El Nurses: A Heritage of Caring at the Foot of Pikes Peak

PROLOGUE

"Nurse…Nurse…Do We Have a Nurse?" has been an anxious call of hospitalized individuals and families living in the community of Colorado Springs since the early days of our founding by General William Jackson Palmer. Community minded, concerned women and men came forward throughout the years to meet the urgent call to establish a general hospital that would provide skilled nursing and medical care. Persons, rich and poor, who suffered from tuberculosis, thronged to Colorado Springs for "fresh air treatment," desperately calling for assistance and care. They were educated, wealthy, and also often socially progressive men and women who came in hopes of recovery from Consumption or White Plague (tuberculosis) that was rampant in crowded cities of the world.

Desperate sufferers arrived by train on General

William Jackson Palmer's Denver and Rio Grande Railroad. General Palmer established the Colorado Springs Hotel in 1872, and later he added the grand Antlers Hotel to welcome hopeful wealthy residents. However, other travelers scraped together just enough to arrive by train or carriage. They required more modest accommodations, as well as food, work, and care for themselves and family members who were in ill health. Citizen entrepreneurs opened their homes, put up tents, and built simple wood structures in an attempt to provide shelter from unexpectedly cold or hot temperatures, often accompanied by wild winds.[2]

Businessmen and doctors, many of whom were also chasing "the cure," opened sanatoriums, built villas, and modest homes on the property sold by General Palmer. Town leaders, prompted by critical needs for medical and nursing care for citizens who became acutely ill with a variety of serious ailments or accidents, quickly set about establishing doctors' offices, mercantile businesses, schools, churches, and other amenities that enhanced the public environment of the city. Wives and women who came west, brought with them an awakening progressive spirit as they saw the desperate needs of fellow citizens. Women of the "Progressive Era," roughly 1880 to 1920, strived to expand the purpose of their lives beyond the confines of the home and their families. For many women, natural social groups were in houses of worship and women's clubs. Women strongly believed they could make a difference in the quality of life for themselves and their fellow citizens.[3]

Mr. D. Russ Wood, who was in ill health, was a wealthy early arrival. He and his wife bought property on Weber Street and hired a local carpenter, Winfield Scott Stratton, to build two villas to accommodate the needs of wealthy invalids. The Woods had three children with "paid help" in the home. As a member of "society," Mrs. Almira Wood (who went by her husband's name only, as was the custom of the time) joined a group of women to assess the community situation. They formed a prudential committee or relief society to focus collective attention on the needs of sick, destitute men, and families. The group quickly elected Mrs. Wood president and revised their name to the Woman's Aid society, a clear statement of the organization's leadership and purpose. The Board changed their name to The Associated Charities in 1899, which identified the group until after World War II.[4]

Like-minded women and other benefactors eagerly contributed to the society in the form of time, energy, and goods, along with whatever funds were available. Mrs. Wood reflected in her article, "A Review of Thirteen Year's Work" published in the *Weekly Gazette,* February 4, 1888,[5] "The object of the society then, as now, was to lend a helping hand when sickness or any calamity befell a family and destitution followed, and also to provide some way that the poor would be able to assist themselves." Mrs. Wood had held the president's chair for 20 years and was in ill health when she retired in 1889. Mrs. Wood developed pneumonia and died in the spring of 1895. At that time, she would have been in her mid-70s.[6]

Mr. William Lennox moved to early Colorado Springs with his parents' family when he was 22 years old. He was an industrious young man, who four years later married Anna (Belle) Cowgill, a young woman from Iowa. Upon arrival in Colorado Springs, she quickly became an eager and dedicated colleague of Mrs. Wood. Her husband, William Lennox, was also anxious to make his mark in the city and took up "...the city fathers on their tree-digging offer. The following year, he gravitated into the feed and hay business, then coal and freight transfer (business), and finally took up mining in Cripple Creek where he became exceedingly wealthy."[7]

Other new residents chasing the cure were a couple, Dr. Samuel Edwin Solly and his wife, Elisabeth (known as Sally), who came from London. Dr. Solly worked to build a luxurious sanatorium, "Cragmor" on Austin Bluffs. Mrs. Solly joined Mrs. Wood and Mrs. Lennox, along with additional colleagues, in the collective goal of making a difference in the health and welfare of less fortunate fellow citizens.[8]

These three women and other dedicated women provided far-reaching leadership in philanthropic endeavors that continue to have a significant influence in the Pikes Peak region today.

Mr. and Mrs. William Lennox were staunch members of the First Methodist Episcopal Church. Belle Lennox's dedicated leadership in community service and church mission endeavors was well known. The Lennox couple developed an enduring relationship. Rev (Dean) Arthur C. Peck and his wife, Mrs. (Frances Potter) Peck, who had previously lived in Colorado Springs. They worked together with the First Methodist Episcopal Church congregation in church and community philanthropic endeavors.[9]

Dean Peck and Mrs. Peck were Denver residents in 1903. He was a highly regarded minister and church fundraiser within the Colorado Conference of the Methodist Episcopal Church. Mrs. Peck was President of the Woman's Home Missionary Society (WHMS) of the Colorado Conference of the Methodist Episcopal Church, headquartered in

Mrs. Frances Potter Peck

Mrs. Peck, an inspired and dedicated Methodist woman, was co-founder of the Colorado Conference Deaconess Hospital. This hospital would become Bethel Hospital and then in 1943, Memorial Hospital.

Mrs. Anna Belle Lennox

Below is the only known small thumbnail image of co-founder, Mrs. Lennox.

Denver. Mrs. Lennox and Mrs. Peck shared an acute awareness of the urgent need for a Protestant hospital to care for the medical health care needs of citizens of all economic situations, not just the folks who were "well off." The women and their husbands, along with their respective organizations, would develop a collaborative plan for which Mrs. Peck became the inspirational spirit and light of the ecumenical humanitarian vision.

Several years earlier, Mrs. (Eleanor Clinton)

Collier and 30 philanthropic minded women had opened a temporary home, the "Eleanor House" (1888–1890), on Weber Street to care for 14 indigent patients. The women, joined by additional compassionate and progressive supporters, requested land from General Palmer to build a building that could accommodate more than Eleanor House could. Palmer complied. Their new building, named Bellevue Sanatorium, was a large, three-story wooden building (see on page 74) on the hill east of the original St. Francis Hospital at East Huerfano Street (Colorado Avenue) and South Institute Street. Three hundred Colorado Springs citizens attended the opening reception on February 13, 1890. The need for care was abundant, but there were many who could not afford to pay for their care and it became financially unfeasible to continue the service, no matter how dedicated the providers.[10] Bellevue Sanatorium closed in 1894.

During the following four years, the building had probably stood empty waiting for another philanthropic group to step up to the challenge. The next ownership effort came from the Methodist Episcopal Deaconess Association, a group of Methodist women headquartered in Chicago who bought the building. They renamed it "National Deaconess Sanatorium," a.k.a. "The New Bellevue Sanatorium." This effort did not have dedicated local support, and it failed. The next interest came from a local group of physicians who incorporated as "The Bellevue Hospital Association," but they also quickly understood the financial difficulties and withdrew their offer in 1903.[11]

By then, the Lennoxes and Pecks knew the struggles of concerned women and community leaders who had attempted to establish sanatoriums for the care of indigent tuberculosis patients. On one pleasant fall afternoon in 1903, Mrs. Lennox and Mrs. Peck were enjoying a drive through Manitou in Mrs. Lennox's little phaeton open carriage. As they drove, they continued their frequent discussions about serious health care dilemmas in Colorado Springs. They discussed their shared vision of a "Deaconess Sanatorium under the direction and care of Deaconess Nurses" to provide hospital care for residents who required general medical, surgical, and obstetric care. Through deep conversations and earnest prayers, they carried their conviction forward. Mrs. Lennox invited Mrs. Peck to address a large number of community women. The ladies, who gathered in the Lennox home, located at 1001 North Nevada Avenue, thoughtfully considered the community's interest in taking up the Protestant hospital cause. After extensive discussions and investigation by the group of women, who represented several Colorado Springs Methodist churches, they asked the Colorado Conference Woman's Home Missionary Society (WHMS) to sponsor the hospital project. The statewide Colorado Conference of the Methodist Episcopal Church joined the women's groups to purchase the former Bellevue property from the Methodist Episcopal Deaconess Association of Chicago. "At Mrs. Peck's request, Bishop H. W. Warren of the Colorado Conference and a leading Methodist layman…secured the property for the Colorado Conference of the Woman's Home Missionary Society (WHMS) in November, 1903."[12]

[2] Eileen Welsome, *Deep Roots, Aspen Pointe and Colorado Springs, Together Since 1875* (Colorado Springs: Aspen Point, 2013), 28, 73.

[3] Dorothy Schneider and Carl J. Schneider, *American Women in the Progressive Era, 1900–1920* (New York : Anchor Books, Doubleday, 1993), 12–19.

[4] Welsome, *Deep Roots*, 14, 30–32, 70.

[5] Almira Wood, "A Review of Thirteen Years Work," *Colorado Springs Weekly Gazette*, February 4, 1888, 6:2-3.

[6] Welsome, *Deep Roots*, 14, 38, 63.

[7] Welsome, *Deep Roots*, 18, 19.

[8] Welsome, *Deep Roots*, 20.

[9] Ollie J. Smith, "Beth-El Woman's Board Yesterday and Today," speech written and delivered by Ollie J. Smith, Secretary of Beth-El Woman's Colorado Springs Board of the Colorado Conference of the Woman's Home Missionary Society of the Methodist Episcopal Church of Colorado Springs, Colorado Springs, 1943. Copy held by Special Collections, Pikes Peak Library District, Colorado Springs.

[10] Manly D. Ormes and Eleanor R. Ormes, *The Book of Colorado Springs* (Colorado Springs: The Dentan Printing Co., 1933), 238.

[11] Sherry L. Nanninga, *Built with Women's Hands: A Deaconess Hospital in Colorado Springs 1904–1912* (Master thesis, Iliff School of Theology, 1994), 1.

[12] Smith, "Beth-El Woman's Board Yesterday and Today," 1.

The Colorado Conference Deaconess Hospital and Training School

915 East Huerfano Street (Colorado Avenue)
1904–1911

The community group formed a local Board of Managers to serve as the local authority for the endeavor. The group asked Mrs. Lennox to assume the presidency, and Mrs. Ollie J. Smith became recording secretary at the request of the members. Mrs. Peck made routine trips from Denver to attend board meetings and always offered the opening prayer. She was a steady, guiding light and an inspirational spirit of their ecumenical and humanitarian vision. Mrs. Peck and Mrs. Lennox were major benefactors, as well as co-founders of a hospital and school of nursing that has continued to serve Colorado Springs today. The first order of business was to choose a name for the facility. Choosing a name proved more difficult than one might expect. Originally, the Colorado Conference

Board of the Woman's Home Missionary Society (WHMS) of the Methodist Episcopal Church chose the name "Colorado Conference Deaconess Sanitarium." The words "sanatorium or sanitarium" were commonly associated with tuberculosis care rather than general hospital care. The Conference (WHMS) Board decided to substitute the name "hospital" which would clearly identify their true mission of care for medical and surgical patients.[13]

The Colorado Conference Deaconess Hospital

The Deaconess Hospital, a three-story wooden structure built in the Dutch Colonial Revival style, stood on top of a treeless hill east of town center. Striped awnings protected porches and entrances from the intense sunshine and wind. White painted latticework below the porch added charm and a feeling of home.

In July 1904, the Conference WHMS Board voted to accept "tuberculosis patients in the earliest stages."[14]

Eventually, as patient numbers increased, the Deaconess Hospital erected five tents on the hospital grounds. The Deaconess local Board of Managers also rented a small house down the hill on Institute Street to serve as a nurses home.[15]

"Old Deaconess" Nursing Staff
We believe the central figures in this formal portrait to be Superintendent Miss Clara Keyhoe, in a white uniform, seated next to Deaconess Mae Adams (dressed in black) as they posed with junior and senior nursing students.[16]

On February 26, 1904, Colorado Conference Deaconess Hospital and Training School opened with Miss Caroline Rotis, a Methodist Deaconess, as superintendent. Emma Deaton arrived in May 1904, to become the director of the hospital. She was a nurse deaconess from the Chicago Training School. In addition to her role as director, she also oversaw one student nurse, who was responsible for daily care of patients. She continued in her role of nurse deaconess at the hospital until Clara Keyhoe arrived to assume the position of superintendent.[17]

Sara Bradshaw, associated with the deaconesses in Denver, came to Colorado Springs to live and work at the hospital in spring 1904. She entered the Deaconess Hospital Training School for Nurses as a probationer nurse to care for the first eight patients. Miss Bradshaw "petitioned the Deaconess Bureau in Denver, [the legal authority of deaconess education] to grant her early graduation in June, 1906; (this was evidently denied) she completed a full three-year course of training and graduated in July, 1907. She was consecrated as a deaconess and moved to Denver the next month."[18]

The Colorado General Assembly created a State Board of Nurse Examiners in 1905, as the eighth state in the Union to adopt standards of nursing practice.[19]

Deaconess Hospital immediately reported they had cared for 140 patients during 1905. Thirty-five cases were acute medical, 38 were chronic medical, with 37 acute surgical, and 30 minor surgical patients. There were 9 births and 10 children admitted. The training school identified 24-class hours of practical nursing skills in the first year, which the nursing director taught. A group of 10 doctors who were the staff physicians taught all the medical subjects.[20]

Mrs. Ollie J. Smith wrote, "On June 12, 1905, a guild was organized to assist in raising funds for the new hospital, to be in cooperation with the local Board of Managers." The guild known as The Protestant Hospital Guild of Colorado Springs was composed of ecumenical progressive-minded women; Mrs. Ira J. Morse elected President; Mrs. W. S. Tarbell, Secretary; and Mrs. Nellie Versteig, Treasurer.[21] (Citizens sometimes referred to the hospital as "The Protestant Hospital.")

The course of instruction at Deaconess Hospital

documented in the State Board report of 1906 included practical nursing, anatomy, and physiology classes. Additional classes were Materia Medica (pharmacology); bacteriology; hygiene; house sanitation; nursing ethics; and philanthropic work, a preparatory course for District (public health) Nursing. Also offered were theoretical courses in obstetrics, care of children, surgical technique, contagious diseases, and care of the nervous and insane. Throughout the three years of training, students had courses and practical experience in the fundamental principles and process of cookery. The students had additional emphasis on food composition and nutritive values of special diets.[22]

Mrs. Lennox and Mrs. Peck's community goal of founding a Protestant hospital under the direction of a deaconess who was a trained nurse was now an actuality. Fundraising responsibilities gathered even more importance.

The community women, Deaconess Hospital Board, and Guild members held bazaars, rummage sales, teas, concerts, benefit baseball games, and chicken pie suppers to raise money. Churches of Colorado Springs held special Thanksgiving offerings and of course, the Hospital Guild held association membership campaigns. Young ladies of the Hospital Guild held "tag days" in the city. Individuals went out with "a contribution box to meet people on the streets, in stores, and offices, at the hotels, and the depots, and asked for support of the hospital, and all who gave had a tag pinned on them." Tag days were a popular means of fundraising for several years.[23]

As patients filled Deaconess Hospital in 1905,

the local Board of Managers, doctors, and community leaders recognized the need for a new building. The board prepared a wish list of improvements for the new hospital. Most important was fireproof construction and level road accessibility for the unpaved streets. Updated patient care facilities and an elevator, which was the latest "have to have" technology, highlighted the list. The Deaconess local Board of Managers identified suitable land at 1400 E. Boulder Street, at the eastern city limit. General William Jackson Palmer agreed to provide a half block of land if the Colorado Conference Deaconess Bureau could raise $50,000 for construction of the new building. "A building committee was appointed by the Colorado Conference Board of the Methodist Episcopal Church consisting of Mr. Wm. Lennox, Mr. Thomas P. Barber, and Mr. E.B. Simmons." Mr. Barber, a locally renowned architect, provided architecture drawings. The Lennoxes raised the money with great personal and community effort.[24]

The Deaconess Hospital annual report, issued in July 1907, reported 16,775 hours of nursing care rendered in the previous year, 672 hours of study, and 4,863 hours of special nursing. All but a very few hospitals of the time structured their offerings in the service/education model. It is clear Miss Bradshaw's additional year of "education" at Deaconess was more about service and providing leadership for younger students than enhancing her nursing knowledge and skill. Clara Keyhoe, a graduate of Sibley Memorial Hospital in Washington D.C., brought additional nursing expertise, along with two additional probationer students who joined the dedicated caregivers. There was a small home on the hospital grounds that served as a nurses home. Eventually, the hospital attained a capacity of 30 patients.[25]

The Colorado Conference Board authorized construction of an all brick, fireproof, H-shaped, three-story hospital in 1906. Unfortunately, three years later money ran out; the unfinished structure would forlornly sit on empty plains at the edge of town until 1909, waiting for financing and direction. (See page 75.) Meanwhile, the Deaconess Hospital local Board of Managers busied themselves with current management concerns and provided for basic needs of the hospital.[26]

Mrs. Lennox served as a dedicated leader of progressive women in Colorado Springs for many years and President of the Deaconess Hospital Board of Managers for five years. Sadly, she died suddenly on April 23, 1909. The grieving Board members formulated a resolution in support of naming the new hospital "The Belle Lennox Deaconess Hospital." Her husband, Mr. William Lennox, declined this request, saying his wife would not want such an honor; however, he continued his solid commitment and financial support of the effort until his death in 1936.[27]

Julia Ray Work, a class of 1913 graduate, and Margaret Glew, class of 1912, captured vivid images of hospital care and training school life at Deaconess Hospital in their 1962 publication, *History of Memorial Hospital and Beth-El School of Nursing*. They reminisced together about the challenges they faced, as well as humorous anecdotes and descriptions of duties beyond comprehension today.

Julia Ray Work (second from left)
with her high-spirited friends in 1910.

Julia's bright eyes and smile gave a hint of her future self. Her congenial nature, commitment to outstanding nursing care, sharp intellect, and positive work ethic led to a 40-year Public Health and School Nursing career in Colorado Springs. By her example and spirit, she inspired generations of schoolchildren, their families, and Beth-El Nurses. Julia was in the Army Nurse Corps, and served in England during World War I. She was a 2004 inductee into The Colorado Nurses Association Hall of Fame.

Photo courtesy of Julia Ray Work, class of 1913.

Their endearing, fun-loving spirit is clear from their shared recollections.

The training school for nurses was started, probably in 1904, as the first class, consisting of one lone nurse who graduated in 1907.

The two local "survivors" of those pioneer training days at "The Old Deaconess," recall with nostalgia the twenty-bed, three-story frame building where patients were carried up and down the stairs "by hand" and where the nurses did everything from stoking the furnace to delivering babies.

The food was hauled up to the floors on a "dumb waiter," which groaned as it ascended and rattled on descent. The kitchen contained a large coal-burning stove. The cook was reliable—but the janitor liked his bottle.

On the grounds, at one side of the hospital, were five tents in which tuberculosis patients were cared for. They received the real fresh air treatment, as snow and wind swept around and in on them. Each tent contained a small coal or wood-burning stove, usually kept going by the nurses. The night nurse, carrying a lantern (lady of the lamp), made frequent trips to these patients, who were usually very ill. Often she would no more than get back up to the third floor than a tent bell would clang again.

The nurses, numbering twelve at the time of this account, lived in houses [nurses home] on South Institute Street, at the foot of the hill. Those houses are still there. The "caste system" prevailed here as the newer nurses were given the kitchens to stay, while the older nurses got the bedrooms and parlors!

This staff of nurses, working in the hospital, did all the cleaning of rooms and halls that often included delirious typhoids [sic] and "delirious" alcoholics who sometimes loved to try to get out of the hospital one way or another.

The hospital superintendent was in charge of the total operation. Third-year students were responsible for patient care and assisted in ward teaching of the younger students and "Probes" [Probationers, or students in their first six months] as they were commonly called. A graduate nurse taught basic nursing arts class; however, ten staff doctors taught all the medical classes. Students worked twelve-hour shifts, seven a.m. to seven p.m., with two hours off—if they were lucky. Classes were held in the afternoons—when possible.[28]

Students completed three years of training and successfully cared for a designated number of "cases" to qualify for graduation and receive a coveted nurse's diploma and the title, "Trained Nurse." The standard of care was good nursing, nourishing food, basic medications, and cleanliness.

In 1909, the Colorado Conference WHMS Board called Florence E. Standish, an extraordinarily talented nurse and deaconess, to come to Colorado Springs to fill the position of Superintendent. Standish graduated from Asbury Methodist Hospital and Rebecca Deaconess Home in Minneapolis, Minnesota. Florence E. Standish, the epitome of a

Progressive Era "New Woman," was a professional woman with a degree, unmarried, and self-supporting. Although Florence never married (sadly, her fiancé died before their marriage), she adopted a premature baby born at Beth-El Hospital in 1912. The tiny baby had little hope, according to doctors; however, Florence moved the baby boy, whom she named Robert, into her hospital superintendent's office to care for him herself. He thrived with her excellent tender care.[29]

Professional progressive women often made careers within the reform movement, as settlement workers, social workers, public health nurses, nursing educators, and hospital superintendents. Miss Standish's solid capabilities and direct approach

Florence E. Standish.

Florence Standish's unique combination of knowledge of nursing, hospital administration, and nursing education, provided a remarkable background from which to make notable contributions to the health of Protestant and ecumenical citizens of Colorado Springs.

Photo courtesy Barbara Standish Lancaster, class of 1941.

proved to be an asset, and perhaps, somewhat of a threat for the earnest, dedicated church-women of the community.[30]

Upon her arrival and installation on October 4, 1909, she found urgent, complex care issues, hospital staff, and training school educational needs. The women of the Deaconess Hospital local Board of Managers, Protestant Hospital Guild, doctors, staff, and people of the community clamored for an elevator in the old hospital. Florence Standish knew that for safe, efficient care immediate attention was required there, but would also be needed in the new hospital once it opened. At this time, the new hospital stood unfinished and unfunded, and appeared almost abandoned on East Boulder Street at the eastern edge of town.

Miss Standish astutely urged the Protestant Hospital Guild to use their elevator fundraising efforts to enhance current care. She listed an upgrade of furnishings and equipment for one large operating room, a sterilizing room, dining room, and kitchen areas of the old hospital. Miss Standish and community fundraising efforts successfully raised almost $5,000, which also provided future funding for furnishing 14 rooms in the new hospital building.[31]

(There are two unsigned documents entitled "History of the School of Nursing of Beth-El Hospital" held by the Colorado State Board of Nursing. Apparently, these reports written in 1928–1930, described this initial elevator fundraising effort as dedicated for the new hospital building rather than Deaconess Hospital. Mrs. Ollie J. Smith, as the local Board of Managers Secretary during this time, is the authentic primary source. Unfortunately, the error in location identification has appeared in previous

Colorado Springs publications.)[32]

"Immediately, Superintendent Standish attained a position not accorded to previous nurses or supervisors. She was voted a member of both the local Deaconess Hospital Board Managers (attending every meeting and participating beyond the usual presentation of the monthly Superintendent's report) and the Conference Deaconess Bureau's committee on applicants."[33]

She revised and enlarged the program of studies, instituted a complete course of practical nursing arts demonstrations, methods, and follow-up work. Patients and doctors of the community gratefully received the success of her venture. Glockner Hospital Training School in Colorado Springs asked her to give demonstration courses to their students, which she gladly provided. At Deaconess Hospital, she also expanded the curriculum and taught courses in history of nursing, hygiene, sanitation, and diet in disease. Florence Standish's educational standards and resulting quality of nursing care established high standards of care, which the citizens of Colorado Springs appreciated and grew to expect.[34]

Miss Standish's professional and collaborative relationships with the community of physicians lead to increased support and recognition of the quality of education at Deaconess Hospital. The Colorado Conference Deaconess Bureau approved a request from Dr. Henry W. Hoagland, Superintendent of Cragmor Sanatorium, situated on Austin Bluffs, for Deaconess students to add a three-month affiliation in tuberculosis nursing at Cragmor. Miss Standish required students to work under a "regularly employed superintendent." As was the business custom of the day, Deaconess Hospital received $40 per month for each student who affiliated with Cragmor.[35]

The second group of four women graduated from the Deaconess Training School in 1909. The third class, consisting of two young women, graduated in 1911.

Mrs. Ollie J. Smith, Recording Secretary of the Deaconess local Board, described the flurry of activity. Women of the Board personally attended to innumerable details of preparing for the new Bethel Hospital's grand opening by wiping windows, sweeping the front hallway, cleaning up the yard, and setting out trees. As Mrs. Smith and Mrs. Vaux share, "finding so much going on up there, they went to their homes, got out their machines and made all the scrim curtains then used for the windows." The women also made dresser scarves, sheets, surgical wraps, and almost any item needed by the hospital staff. Their effort was a true *women's work of love.*[36]

Julia Ray Work Holding Baby c1915

Julia is taking in the sunshine with an infant outside of the hospital. Note the car parked in the background where Boulder Park now is.

[13] Smith, "Beth-El Woman's Board Yesterday and Today," 3.

[14] Colorado Conference Woman's Home Missionary Society, Book of Minutes III, July 5, 1904, 221.

[15] Nanninga, *Built with Women's Hands,* 33.

[16] Nanninga, *Built with Women's Hands*, 50.

[17] Nanninga, *Built with Women's Hands*, 31.

[18] Nanninga, *Built with Women's Hands*, 41.

[19] National League of Nursing Education, *Standard Curriculum for School of Nursing Committee on Education*, (Baltimore: Waverly Press, 1919), 59.

[20] Deaconess Hospital Training School, *Colorado State Board of Nurse Examiners*, Report filed c1906.

[21] Smith, "Beth-El Woman's Board Yesterday and Today," 2.

[22] Deaconess Hospital Training School "Colorado State Board of Nurse Examiners," Report filed c1906 with the Colorado State Board of Nursing.

[23] Deaconess Bureau of the Woman's Home Missionary Society of the Colorado Conference of the Methodist Episcopal Church, Minutes, August 31, 1908.

[24] Smith, "Beth-El Woman's Board Yesterday and Today," 3.

[25] Nanninga, *Built with Women's Hands*, 31, 41, 43.

[26] Nanninga, *Built with Women's Hands*, 40–47.

[27] Local Board Minutes Book 2, Local Board of the Woman's Home Missionary Society of the Colorado Springs Methodist Episcopal Church, Colorado Springs, May 3, 1909.

[28] Julia R. Work and Margaret Glew, *History of*

Memorial Hospital and Beth-El School of Nursing 1904–1963 (Colorado Springs: Beth-El Alumnae Association, 1963), 3.

[29] Barbara Lancaster Standish and Robert Standish, interview by Joanne F. Ruth, Colorado Springs, July 9, 1983.

[30] National Women's History Museum, "Reforming Their World: Women in the Progressive Era," http://www.nwhm.org/online-exhibits/progressiveera/statuswomenprogressive.html (accessed August 26, 2014).

[31] Smith, "Beth-El Woman's Board Yesterday and Today," 2, 3.

[32] Joanne F. Ruth, "Explaninary Note," Colorado Springs, December 2014.

[33] Nanninga, *Built with Women's Hands*, 52.

[34] Joanne F. Ruth conversations with daughter, Barbara Standish Lancaster, Colorado Springs, 1983–2014.

[35] "Colorado Conference Deaconess Bureau, Secretary's Book of the Supervisory Committee of the Deaconess Home," Denver: Methodist Episcopal Church, November 29, 1909.

[36] Smith, "Beth-El Woman's Board Yesterday and Today," 5.

Beth-El Hospital and Training School

1400 East Boulder Street
1911–1922

Beth-El Hospital 1922

Beth-El Hospital featured steps leading up to the formal front door. Open porches located at the south end of the east wing and along hallways connecting the two wings provided a quiet retreat for patients and visitors. A bench in front of the hospital was a comfort for passengers who waited for the Boulder Street streetcar.

The formal dedication occurred on July 2, 1911. The Colorado Conference WHMS Board chose the name "Bethel Hospital" for the new building. In 1909, Mrs. Peck proposed the Hebrew name "Bethel," which means House of God, for the long-awaited facility.[37] At this time, she wrote an inspirational poem and hymn "Bethel, House of God," which expressed the years of sustained commitment by volunteers and benefactors and her fervent hope for the future of the noble mission.[38] The Deaconess Bureau Board minutes of June 26, 1911, recorded a change in the word "Bethel" to include a hyphen and capital E, which the board felt more closely adhered to the old Hebrew form of the word Beth-El.[39] (The two variations in the spelling were almost interchangeable for many years.) The planning committee enthusiastically featured the hymn during the dedication service. The Colorado Conference WHMS Board had a large brass plaque struck with the Bethel poem and had it hung adjacent to the Superintendent's door in the hospital front corridor.[40]

Bethel

Bethel, "The House of God," its name:
Thine may it ever truly be!
A place of holy ministries,
A sacred dwelling, shared by Thee!
Thy Presence ever fill this house!
Thy love be ever manifest
To all who come within these doors,
And weary suff'rers here find rest!

The University of Colorado Colorado Springs (UCCS) Archives displays the original brass plaque at Beth-El College of Nursing and Health Sciences.

Patients and nurses moved in on July 3, 1911. Student nurses lived on the third floor of the administration or west wing until 1916, when the Nurses Home opened. Students wore newly designed uniforms, which reflected the latest fashion of the day. Dresses were full-length blue chambray, featuring long sleeves, starched white apron, bib, collar and large cuffs, with the newly adopted "Beth-El cap." Black hose and high buttoned or laced shoes completed their professional appearance. Students wore no makeup or curls in their hair. Their hair could not touch the stiff white collar while on duty.[41] The nursing administration considered it mandatory that students did not allow the cuffs of their uniform to become wet, dirty nor have the cuffs rolled up.

The new building was safer, easier to drive to, and had a larger capacity with 80 beds; however, the

Student Nurses Gather on a Sun Porch
A black velvet strip on cap indicated Senior student status.

number of available nurses and students did not necessarily increase. Physicians continued to be the primary lecturers for the students. Graduate nurses served as supervisors of the various departments, and students staffed the hospital 24 hours a day. The nursing director scheduled physicians' lectures and nursing classes in the afternoon or evening after patient morning care was finished. Students returned from class to the wards to serve dinner trays and administer bedtime care. All students provided individual patient nursing care; however, the junior and senior students also served as charge nurses for 12-hour shifts, both day and night. The students prepared and mixed medications, prepared special diet foods, sterilized instruments, prepared all medical procedure trays. They folded linens, cleaned the wards, and much more in the name of gaining experience as well as providing service to the hospital mission.

Although caring for the ill was much easier in the new Beth-El Hospital, the linens still had to be soaked in bathtubs that sometimes resulted in an overflow and a frantic time of mopping. Students also continued to carry covered bedpans down the hall to empty in the central utility room. Personal photo albums of early Beth-El graduates clearly show the dedication they felt for patients and hospital. The workdays were long, but they found time to relax. They recorded their delight of being a part of this new hospital and personal adventures in their photos. They enjoyed the prospect of becoming "a graduate nurse."[42]

A favorite location for both clinical work and

relaxation was with the children cared for in the Visiting Nurse Association Children's Ward. The inpatient facility was located on the first floor, east wing of the hospital. The Children's Pavilion, a small wooden building, situated on the northeast corner of the Beth-El property was open-air housing. A discussion of the purpose and historical details of these children's facilities appears as an addendum to this book. (See page 143.)

Children's Pavilion

Separate open-air sleeping porches for girls and boys flanked the central dining hall and nurse's office.

Courtesy Julia Ray Work collection.

The school, now proudly known as Beth-El Hospital Training School, graduated seven proud young women in 1912. The program listed staff of the Beth-El Hospital as Florence E. Standish, Superintendent; Lois L. Shardlow, Supervisor of Nurses. Also listed were Betty H. Gardner, Head Surgical Nurse; Juliet A. Farr, Anesthetist; and Eva R. Keech. Mrs. A. C. Peck presided over the formal ceremony and Florence E. Standish administered a modified version of the "Hippocratic Oath." Upon graduation, the women received organdy caps, which replaced muslin caps worn by students. Only students and graduates of Beth-El Hospital Training School (and later School of Nursing) wore this unique cap. They also received a newly designed round gold graduate pin. The Deaconess graduate pin, which featured a red cross design, probably provided the basic form for the new nurses pin.[43] The new pin also had a red cross and white enamel ring with the words Beth-El Hospital Training School encircling the cross. Initials W. H. M. S. (Woman's Home Missionary Society) appeared as one letter at the end of each arm of the cross. The number 12 was placed in the center of the cross to signify the year of their graduation.[44] (See page 126.)

Experiences and education of Beth-El Training School students were similar to most schools across the United States. The National League of Nursing Education, under the leadership of M. Adelaide Nutting, Director of Nurses at Teachers College, New York City, continued in their effort to enhance nursing care offered to the public through improved educational standards for student nurses. Miss Nutting observed the following in her introduction to their 1919 publication, *Standard Curriculum for Schools of Nursing:*

> The purpose, which the Committee has had in view, is to arrive at some general agreement as to a desirable and workable standard whose main features could be accepted by training schools of good standing throughout the country. In this

way, it is hoped that we may be able to gradually overcome the wide diversity of standards at present existing in schools of good standing throughout the country…. She [the graduate] must be ready to serve the whole community and to meet conditions as she finds them in many different communities.[45]

Graduates filled with professional pride naturally desired to maintain their sisterhood and lifelong friendships, which evolved through shared experiences in the training school. In 1913, the Beth-El Alumnae Association formed with Miss Minnie Isensee, class of 1912, as President. Their objective at this time was social; however, being a member of a formal school alumnae became the next logical professional step.[46] Training School Alumnae

1924 Beth-El Alumnae Association

The Alumnae have provided strong and steady professional leadership in the lives of students, School of Nursing, Beth-El Hospital, and residents of Colorado Springs.

Association membership became mandatory for membership in the State (Nurses) Association. This membership provided automatic membership in the National (Nurses) Association. Alumnae Association membership soon became almost mandatory for all graduates from Schools of Nursing in the United States.

The mission of the organization expanded quickly to become a strong supportive presence for Beth-El School of Nursing. The graduates were also of the progressive spirit and were ready to express their caring and community spirit.

Graduates had limited choices of nursing positions. In the early years, Beth-El Hospital hired only four or five graduate nurses in leadership positions. The remaining graduates competed for the limited available options, which only allowed them to be a "special" nurse (private duty), public health nurse, school nurse, or supervisor in a hospital. If a graduate married, she "lost" her identity and was listed only by her husband's name, which was reflected in a record of alumni from 1907 to 1916. [47]

There was a great need for private duty nurses; however, the cost of a special nurse was out of reach for a great majority of families. Many graduate nurses who wished to work could not find employment. There was a somewhat hidden explanation for this sad situation. During the early years of the twentieth century, small communities throughout Colorado and the nation each had their small hospital operated by an independent physician. The primary objective of these hospitals was to find affordable (not paid) help to care for the "in-house" patients. Most hospitals could offer only the most basic "hospital training" for student nurses, with only a few graduate-prepared nurses on the staff.

Citizens recognized the value of public health nurses; however, few nurses had advanced knowledge required for this almost independent nursing role. The Committee for the Study of Nursing Education, funded by the Rockefeller Foundation, focused attention on the lack of public health nursing education in a study initiated in 1919. As an outcome of this work, Rockefeller Foundation financed Yale University School of Nursing, which successfully demonstrated the educational and public value of an endowed professional nursing school in 1923.[48]

With this bit of background into the development of nursing education and nursing practice, let us return to the flow of education at Beth-El Training School. Following a series of meetings and communications between the Beth-El local Board of Managers and the Conference WHMS and Florence Standish, the relationship was beginning to fray. There are no official public records of the concerns; however, Florence E. Standish resigned from Beth-El Hospital in September 1912. She had begun to build a home on a large tract of land at 319 Logan Street earlier in the year. This house was the first house built near the hospital on the south side of Boulder Street. Miss Standish founded a tuberculosis sanatorium, Nob Hill Lodge, on her property. (See page 78.) She was the only professional woman and nurse who owned and managed a comprehensive tuberculosis sanatorium in a city filled with sanatoriums. She had gained deep respect and loyal support from physicians in the community, which continued throughout her lifetime. Her former colleague, Lois Shardlow built a home-style sanatorium next door to Nob Hill.[49]

At the start of what would be known as the Great War (World War I), Miss Standish received a commission in the Army Nurse Corps. She was requested to utilize her extraordinary nursing and administrative skills to open and direct a large Army hospital at Oteen, North Carolina. In a very unusual move for the time, she returned to Colorado Springs to take her young son, Robert, with her to North Carolina. Following her service, she returned to Colorado Springs and Nob Hill Lodge. After the war, the Army contracted with Miss Standish to care for tubercular veterans at Nob Hill Lodge. In the summer of 1920, Florence unexpectedly adopted a second child, a five-week-old baby girl, Barbara Rose. Miss Standish chose her name in honor of Miles Standish's two wives. (Florence's family history indicated she was a direct descendant of Miles Standish.) In 1925, Miss Standish contracted diphtheria of the "paralytic type" and almost died. She recovered enough to travel and live near her sister Helen, who was also a nurse and lived in California. Florence E. Standish sold The Nob Hill Lodge Sanatorium at that time. Later she moved back to Colorado Springs with her family, though her health remained fragile. Excerpts from a class newsletter edited in February 1937 by Mabel E. Smith, class of 1912, brought Beth-El Alumnae up to date with Miss Standish's activities. Miss Standish wrote, "The years have also brought me much happiness and joy, as well as opportunities to be of service to others, for all of which I am duly grateful."[50]

Florence's daughter, Barbara, graduated from Colorado Springs High School and entered Beth-El School of Nursing in 1939. When her mother's health failed and she could no longer live in her home, Dr. E. John Brady invited Florence to live in a convalescent room at Brady Hospital in Colorado Springs. Florence E. Standish died in 1941, just before Barbara graduated from Beth-El School of Nursing.

Beth-El Nurses Home
1508 East Boulder Street
1916–1973

Beth-El Nurses Home
Students originally lived on the third floor, west wing of the Beth-El Hospital building until the nurses' home opened in 1916. The Nurses Home was the hub of student life for 56 years.

General Palmer's Colorado Springs Company donated half a block of land on Boulder Street, east of the hospital, for an urgently needed Nurses Home and Training School building. The two-story building, which had a basement and buff-colored brick, was located at 1508 East Boulder Street. Located on the first floor were the parlor, director of nurses room, and student rooms. (See page 79.) Additional student rooms occupied the second floor with a total capacity of 52 students. The basement held classrooms, an overflow dormitory room, utility room, and eventually a nursing arts laboratory.

1920 Classroom in Nurses Home

Student uniforms, made by their mothers, were required dress for class, and also anytime they were in the hospital to work or eat in the dining room. Hospital expansion plan in 1973 required the aging Nurses Home demolished to make way for a planned parking structure. Memorial Hospital built a large Children's Hospital on this location in 2007.

Observation Hospital Building
(City/County)
427 North Foote Avenue
1918–1973

For years, the cities and counties had attempted several strategies to care for primarily poor citizens who suffered from contagious diseases (other than tuberculosis) or mental health problems. The state of Colorado addressed this problem by a mandate for cities and counties to provide facilities for the health and safety of all citizens. Observation Hospital was the local solution. Through the years, it fulfilled this basic stopgap mission. As the need arose, the mission and name changed to Contagion Hospital, then Memorial Annex, Beth-El Senior Dorm, and lastly, Beth-El School of Nursing.[51]

Present-day citizens have probably lost memory of Observation Hospital; however, Beth-El students who worked, lived, or studied in the building during its 56 years of existence, remember it with mixed feelings. In 1917, after considerable citizen discussion, physicians along with city and county officials decided to obtain a small portion of land north of Beth-El Hospital at 427 Foote Avenue. Collaboratively, El Paso County and Colorado Springs funded and built a modest, two-story brick building with basement, that was primarily a contagion hospital with one small section dedicated to the care of the insane.[52]

The building was completed and furnished, ready for the official opening on October 1, 1918. The worldwide epidemic of Spanish Influenza struck young soldiers who were studying radio operations at Colorado College. On September 28, Observation

Hospital opened and sprang into action. Unfortunately, the next day, September 29, a young soldier died at Beth-El Hospital from lobar pneumonia, which followed the influenza.[53]

Ruth Penney, Beth-El class of 1919, was eighty-eight years old in 1983 when she shared her vivid memory of Armistice Day, November 11, 1918.

> The eleventh month and the eleventh day, the devastating World War [World War I] ended with the signing of the Armistice by our President Woodrow Wilson and European diplomats. The long siege of fighting was over; we had waited and prayed for this news. Thousands of our boys were in the conflict, on the front lines, living, suffering, and dying.
>
> At home, we had meatless and wheatless days—women were busy knitting socks, gloves, and scarves for our soldiers in those long winter months of fighting. The government was selling War Bonds. We had passed through that new deadly plague, called influenza. The doctors were puzzled and frightened, for treatment and medication had little effect—the death rate from this pestilence was high.
>
> This November 11, 1918, I was a senior nurse at Bethel Hospital, Colorado Springs, Colorado. The morning had started as usual—roll call, breakfast, nursing assignment. I

was assigned to the operating room, but no surgery was listed for that day. Suddenly, the world outside of the hospital was full of noise and excitement. Word had come by telegraph and telephone (no radio or television in 1918) that the Armistice had been signed, the fighting in this World War had ceased—the news we had waited so long to hear.

The whole world was celebrating: church bells were ringing, and whistles were blowing, people running into the streets, crying, shouting and singing. Some of us nurses joined the crowd in our excitement and were soon down in the center of town where a parade had started. Trucks and cars full of people joined in the parade led by a band. All the Model-T Fords and cars were tooting their horns while the band played, "Over There, Over There," and "When Johnny Comes Marching Home," "A Long Way to Tipperary," and "The National Anthem." Flags were flying everywhere. Our boys were coming home; then the sad thought: many would not return.

No segregation that day; all ages and nationalities mingled, shouted, laughed, and rejoiced together. The runaway nurses watched the parade for a short time, then hurried back to the hospital. We had left without permission and wondered what awaited us—we could have been expelled. No surgery had been scheduled in our absence; no questions were asked. We went back to work still very excited.

I graduated from nursing training in 1919, not to nursing in army barracks or a foreign soil, but in the U.S.A.[54]

Esther Tandy Paden, class of 1920, commented that there were no planned activities off duty during the war years; however, "someone donated a piano to the new nurses home and we used to do a lot of singing around it. ... And one more thing, we had brains and eggs every Wednesday."[55]

Esther's classmate, Freda Morris Disch, remembered an extraordinary patient, Mr. Nakamura.

Beth-El at one time had TB patients. [Apparently, there remained only a few TB patients and they had not been housed within the Beth-El Hospital building.] When I entered Training School, Naky was the only T.B. patient left. All year he slept on the open porch [in front of a hallway between the east and west wings], and he "cleared" [coughed up sputum] as he called it, faithfully. If we were busy and forgot his nourishment at 10:00 a.m. and 3:00 p.m., he stood by the diet kitchen door until someone had a moment to fix his chocolate malted milk. I believe it was 1918 or 1919 when he became well enough to return to Japan. His plans were made and his trunk packed. Having "recovered," he was given permission to go into town, which he did. He apparently became overtired and caught the flu, and in less than a week, he had passed away.[56]

1919 Student Nurses with "Naky" Pose in the Operating Room

Inventive in their off-duty time, students enjoyed taking pictures with their Kodak "Brownie" box cameras. The natural light from the north facing operating room windows provided an excellent opportunity to document a light-hearted moment with their patient and friend Mr. Nakamura. They are wearing hospital OR scrub uniforms. Courtesy Pikes Peak Library District.

In 1919, the Colorado Conference WHMS Board recognized the enormous responsibility the women of the Beth-El local Board of Management (as it was then known) experienced in the management of a growing hospital, training school, and fundraising all at the same time. The Colorado Conference WHMS Board reformed the leadership structure of the hospital. They elected a new men's Board of Managers to manage routine hospital affairs. This board consisted of Dr. W. W. Flora, President; Mr. E. B. Simmons, Secretary; and Mr. Wm. Lennox, Treasurer. Included later was the pastor of the First Methodist Episcopal Church of Colorado Springs. These gentlemen were the husbands of core leaders of the previous Beth-El local Board of Management. The dedicated women, who adopted the name of Women's Board of Beth-El, dedicated their energies to raising money, gifts for the maintenance and future support of the hospital. Mrs. Peck remained wholeheartedly dedicated to the hospital and training school. (One of her granddaughters, Margaret [Peg] Barnes, class of 1927, was a Beth-El School of Nursing graduate). Mrs. Peck died in Denver, following a major operation September 13, 1930.[57]

It was not long before the Colorado Conference of the Methodist Episcopal Church and Woman's Home Missionary Society of the Colorado Conference were holding conversations with the National Board of Hospitals, Homes, and Deaconess Work of the Methodist Episcopal Church. December 18, 1922, the women gave the hospital to the national board. This gift, "valued at a quarter of a million dollars" was the largest gift ever made by a Woman's Society to the board of the church."[58]

Children's Hospital School of Nursing in Denver and Beth-El School of Nursing established a collaborative exchange of student affiliation in 1921.

Beth-El nurses went to Denver for three months for instruction and experience in pediatrics and orthopedic nursing. Children's Hospital students came to Beth-El for nine months of education and experience in adult medical/surgical nursing. The Children's nurses wore white uniforms with pink dresses under their bibs and aprons; of course, they gained the nickname, "Pinkies." This exchange provided an opportunity for students to have broader pediatric care opportunities and experience another hospital culture. The affiliation continued until 1963.

Beth-El Nursery Nurses and Dr. Timmons with "their babies." 1920

Beth-El was renowned for their excellent care of mothers and babies. Standard practice of the day required a woman to stay in the hospital ten days following the birth of her baby.

[37] Local Board of Managers Minutes Book 2, September 1, 1909.

[38] Frances E. Peck, "Beth-El" words and music transcribed by Linda Ellis Cummings from vocal recollection and recording by Irene Hall, class of 1932. Sheet music available, Beth-El Alumni Collection, University of Colorado Colorado Springs (UCCS) Archives.

[39] Deaconess Bureau minutes, June 26, 1911.

[40] Local Board of Managers Minutes Book 2, May 3, 1909.

[41] Freda Morris Disch, *Beth-El Alumni Questionnaire*, Beth-El Alumni Collection Binder 1920, Beth-El Alumni Collection, (UCCS)Archives.

[42] Marjorie Henderson Martin, "Alumni Scrapbooks 1973, Vol. I, II" Colorado Springs: Beth-El Alumni Association.

[43] Nanninga, *Built with Women's Hands*, 53.

[44] "1912 Graduation Program," Beth-El Training School, Colorado Springs.

[45] M. Adelaid Nutting, Introduction, *Standard Curriculum for Schools of Nursing* by the Committee on Education of the National League of Nursing Education (Baltimore: Waverly Press, 1919), 5.

[46] Beth-El Yearbook Committee, *TPR* Beth-El Yearbook (Colorado Springs: Beth-El School of Nursing, 1930), 82.

[47] "History of Beth-El School of Nursing," paper held by Colorado State Board of Nursing (Colorado Springs: Beth-El School of Nursing, 1928).

[48] Josephine Goldmark, *Nursing and Nursing Education*

in the United States (New York: The MacMillan Company, reprinted by Garland Publishing, 1923, reprinted 1984), 7–30.

[49] Nanninga, *Built with Women's Hands*, 60.

[50] Florence E. Standish, letter, "Round Robin" Alumni Newsletter, 1937, 3.

[51] Welsome, *Deep Roots*, 33, 76.

[52] Ormes, *The Book of Colorado Springs*, 260.

[53] Katie Rudolph, "The Influenza Pandemic of 1918: A Colorado Springs Timeline" in *Doctors, Disease, and Dying in the Pikes Peak Region*, ed. Tim Blevins, et al., (Colorado Springs: Pikes Peak Library District, 2012), 307.

[54] Ruth E. A. Penney, "Memory of Armistice Day, November, 11, 1918" Binder 1918, Beth-El Alumni Collection, UCCS Archives.

[55] Esther Tandy Paden, "Beth-El Alumni Questionnaire" Binder 1920, Beth-El Alumni Collection, UCCS Archives.

[56] Freda Morris Disch, "Beth El Alumni Questionnaire" Addendum, Binder 1920, Beth-El Alumni Collection, UCCS Archives.

[57] Smith, "Beth-El Woman's Board Yesterday and Today," 4.

[58] Florence Peck, "History of Beth-El Hospital," *TPR* Beth-El Yearbook, (Colorado Springs: Beth-El School of Nursing, 1923), 11.

Beth-El General Hospital

1400 East Boulder Street
1922–1943

1929 Beth-El General Hospital

The fireproof building featured all brick exterior and interior walls. Reconstruction in 1977–1979 surrounded the two original wings of the hospital with a new brick façade. The front and rear courtyards were removed. The original roofline and buff brick walls are visible from the patient tower, south facing windows of the sixth floor. The tower stands on the footprint of 1918 Observation Hospital. — "Beth-El Hospital is still in there."

The hospital name changed to Beth-El General Hospital to recognize its expanding health care purposes. The hospital used the term Department of Nursing Education; however, Beth-El School of Nursing was the formal name preferred by faculty, students, and alumnae. Many community folks continued to use more familiar terms of "training school" or "nurses training" for many years to come.

Opel Stanford Rutherford, class of 1922, talked with Jean Johns, Director, about her days at Beth-El Training School. Johns reported:

> Students in her classes had one half days per week off and worked twelve hours shifts or more, depending if the work was done. The students helped to staff the hospital, and if too many emergency patients or deliveries occurred, students were expected to stay until the work was under control. Her day started at seven a.m., preceded by attending prayers. If she was late, she had to give up breakfast because there was not the time for both prayers and breakfast. Prayers were held in the school parlors. At one time when she asked the director if she would get to go to church, the Director (Esther O. West R.N.) said "yes" she could go with her. That did not help, as Opel wanted to go with a date.[59]

National Methodist Episcopal Sanatorium for Tuberculosis

1532 East Boulder Street

1926–1943

The large windows seemed to provide a wall of sparkling light and sunshine. An elevator provided convenient access to the sunroof for open-air sunbaths and inspiring mountain views.

Architect Mr. Thomas P. Barber drew plans for the proposed million-dollar National Methodist Episcopal Sanatorium for Tuberculosis on 29 acres of property at the corner of East Boulder Street and North Union Boulevard. The building located at 1532 East Boulder Street was the first and only building completed on the property. The men of the National Board of Hospitals and Homes of the Methodist Episcopal Church held a grand formal dedication November 9, 1926. The four-story sanatorium cost $325,000. Mr. Barber designed the fireproof four-story brick building with a finished basement especially for the care of TB patients. The "San" as the students called it, had large south-facing windows in all the patient rooms. There was a promenade deck on the roof for mandatory, daily fresh air and sun treatments for most of the 52 patients. A concrete 730-foot tunnel connected the main hospital, or "Administration Building," with the sanatorium. This concrete tunnel provided a passageway for steam and service pipes from the heating plant and laundry, as well as transport of food, linens, a walkway for staff, and when required, patients.[60]

Beth-El faculty reflected their optimism of the previous decade in the 1930 yearbook:

> The Training School for Nurses is outstanding in its policy of social and athletic activities for the students as may be seen by the various school organizations. Good times thus afforded the nurses, in many ways, to make the hospital and classroom work much easier. Beth-El authorities believe in play in its proper place, and the nurses of Beth-El appreciate this policy.[61]

Society of the Roaring '20s promoted a more active lifestyle for young women. With this socially acceptable new lifestyle, high schools and YWCAs (Young Women's Christian Association) were organizing basketball teams. Nursing schools expanded opportunities for students to participate in broader social activities. In 1923, students published their first yearbook, *T.P.R.* (Temperature, Pulse, and Respiration). A basketball team formed and practiced at the YWCA in 1925. Students had long enjoyed singing around the piano in the Nurses Home parlor, so it was natural to form a glee club in 1925 with Mr. Stanley Effinger, a local music teacher, as director.

Irene Neese Hall, class of 1932, a member of the glee club, remembered they sang the Bethel hymn, written by Mrs. Peck, as a benediction for each concert they performed. During a 1992 alumni luncheon/meeting, the women were recalling early school traditions. As Irene thought of their many concerts, she unexpectedly began to sing this treasured hymn. Later she recorded both stanzas of the hymn.

1931 Beth-El Glee Club

Members of the Glee Club paused for a formal portrait in the parlor of the Nurses Home. The classic Beth-El student uniform was designated the official Glee Club concert uniform. In the midst of the dark days of the Depression and Dust Bowl, their many concerts brought a sense of hope to weary and discouraged families.

Courtesy of Sally Moody Brawner, class of 1933.

Linda Ellis Cummings of Colorado College arranged and transcribed the music. A chance conversation over lunch returned a treasured Beth-El symbol to the collective memory of students, alumni, and the community.[62] The 1994 Gerontology Nursing students invited the alumni to a special recognition luncheon in 1992. The students learned the Beth-El Hymn and sang it as a unique gift of love and honor for alumni.[63]

Beth-El

The hymn below is Linda Cummings' arrangement. She created this transcription by listening to Irene Hall's recording and transcribing what she heard and adding accompaniment.

Idlewold Nurses Home
311 North Logan Avenue
1928–1952

Idlewold Senior Dorm

Senior students slept on the open porches just as the former TB patients; however, the students enjoyed the feeling of "home" as they developed their personal and professional confidence. Since 1984, this building, as the Ronald McDonald House of Southern Colorado, continues to welcome and support families whose seriously ill children receive medical treatment at hospitals in Colorado Springs.

Idlewold Sanatorium (owned by Lois Shardlow, a former Beth-El supervisor) at 311 North Logan Avenue, was bought by the hospital and converted into a dormitory in 1928. The building became known simply as Idlewold or Senior Nurses Home. Mary Kay Smith, Director of Nursing and the School of Nursing, had a room and served as housemother.

Mr. Guy Hanner, hospital administrator (1921–1941), maintained an ever-watchful eye on the budget. Generous benefactors supported Beth-El General

Hospital through the years, including individuals, church groups, or citizens' clubs. In the *Beth-El Hospital Bulletin* published December 1929, Mr. Hanner recognized individual gifts from 15 groups from all over the state of Colorado. Donors gave linens (gowns, diapers, shirts, sheets, pillowcases, and dresser scarves) for use of the patients and hospital. Women in Greeley and Denver Methodist churches organized 50 individual Beth-El Hospital Guilds with the goal of building support for the hospital. Mr. Hanner, of course, accepted "Free Service Fund," donations sent directly to the Hospital. "Women also assisted in making the annual 'egg shower' and 'fruit shower' a success." They held all the usual bazaars, teas, and socials to raise much-needed funds. The hospital wish list included such diverse endeavors as painting rooms and buying dishes, obtaining drapes and a kitchen range, and enacting noise control (doorstops and checks). The list continued with a cystoscopic table, furniture, a general fixtures fund, a new operating room, and lastly, $40,000 for a new Nurses Home. Methodist youth groups brought in gifts such as home canned fruits, honey, and vegetables of many kinds.[64]

Another fundraising effort had been in place for some time. Mr. Hanner mounted Honorary Brass Room Door Plates on the outside or inside of patient room doors. A plaque on the outside of a door represented a $1,000 donation while an inside door plaque represented a $300 gift. Donors and the hospital highly valued the honor of these brass plates.[65]

Mr. Hanner did not think to mention in his Christmas publication the many individuals who were the most outstanding ambassadors of the hospital and

its caring mission. These were the 72 students
enrolled in Beth-El School of Nursing. Students gave
expert nursing care to patients. They prepared diet
trays, assembled procedure trays, cleaned rooms after
patient discharge, as well as untold additional tasks
"as needed" around the hospital.

Students who joined the Glee Club and
Basketball Team traveled many weekends a year, to
towns all over the front range and beyond. These
idealistic young women, just by their presence,
demonstrated a well-rounded vision of healthy,
intellectual, and caring women who were on their way
to a proud profession. With their visits to churches
and schools, they planted seeds of hope for the
future. The real bonus for the hospital was the role
these students played in the recruitment of patients,
student nurses, and of course, financial donations to
Beth-El General Hospital.[66]

These excursions were also an opportunity to
encourage talented high school students to come to
Beth-El so they too could join the basketball team or
glee club. Each traveling student was required to
make up all lost hours of hospital duty and missed
classes even if it eventually delayed their graduation
date. The students who were not members of the
traveling groups were required to take up the slack in
patient care hours while their classmates were away.
Unfortunately, they did not have other opportunities
for recreation or relaxation. With this in mind, they all
participated in uncounted hours of public relations,
which enhanced the financial stability of Beth-El
General Hospital. State Board of Nursing Examiners
were told these trips were enrichment and recreational
opportunities; however, the Examiners questioned

the unusual number of hours required by the extracurricular program and undoubtedly questioned the primary purpose of the activities.[67] The national report, *Nursing and Nursing Education in the United States* (Secretary Josephine Goldmark compiled the report), published for the Study of Nursing Education in 1923, provided a spotlight on similar concerns regarding the quality of nursing, nursing education, hospitals, and healthcare across the nation.[68]

Following the "Goldmark report," the *TPR* Beth-El yearbook of 1926 announced, "The State Board of Nurse Examiners of Colorado has recently recommended that the Standard Curriculum as outlined by the National League of Nursing Education be adopted by all the schools of Nursing of Colorado. The Beth-El School of Nursing has adopted the Standard Curriculum…as far as its adoptability seems possible." The yearbook included the newly adopted three-year curriculum plan.[69]

Nationally, The Committee on the Grading of Nursing Schools formed to assess opportunities to improve the quality of nursing, increase the quantity, and lower the cost. The committee launched a three-phase national study process in the fall of 1926. (This massive nursing study followed publication of the "Flexner report," the report by Abraham Flexner that described the current state of medical education and practice, and was published as *The Carnegie Foundation for the Advancement of Teaching: Medical Education in the United States and Canada,* Bulletin Number 4, 1910.) The Committee on Grading of Nursing Schools was composed of representatives of nursing, medical, and hospital organizations as well as a few educational and lay members. Dr. William Darrach, a well-known surgeon, was chairman. Dr. May Ayres Burgess, an educator, psychologist, and statistician, directed this major study. Beth-El School of Nursing was one of the 2,205 schools of nursing invited to participate in the study. The committee collected and analyzed monthly data and ranked results, confidentially marked, so only an individual school and hospital would know their results in each of the assessment reports. Individual reports were: *Results of the First Grading Study of Nursing, Section I*—The supply and demand for graduate nurses, a "job analysis" of what nurses do, distributed in 1930; *Section II—What Students Learn*, distributed February 1931; *Section III— Who Controls the School?*, distributed, April 1931. *The Second Grading of Nursing Schools*, published results based on data gathered from schools of nursing in the United States during the year 1932. (UCCS Archives holds Beth-El's reports, Section II, and Section III). A primary recommendation was for the National League of Nursing Education to undertake the accreditation of nursing schools. The Committee published their conclusions in three major books. *Nurses, Patients and the Pocketbooks*, 1928; *An Activity Analysis of Nursing*, 1934; and *Nursing Schools Today and Tomorrow*, 1934.[70]

During Christmas of 1929, the administration of Beth-El General Hospital did not know it would become exponentially more difficult to continue serving new mothers, sick children, ill adults, and infirmed elders of Colorado Springs and Colorado. The Depression and Dust Bowl of the 1930s would consume their lives in the lean months and years ahead.

Citizens, Protestant and ecumenical, who lived at

the foot of the mountains and on the high plains of Colorado, had come to rely on medical and nursing care received at Beth-El. At this time, farming provided a broad economic base for Colorado's communities. A weather pattern during the 1920s brought more rain than usual, and crops grew; farmers worried about severe hailstorms and prairie fires that followed lighting strikes. The Great War (WW I) and Spanish Influenza left scars on individual family life, but communities coped and continued to thrive. The predictability of life changed drastically in 1929 when the stock markets crashed around the world. In the early 1930s, the weather began to change on the Great Plains. Previously predictable rains no longer fell; however, the winds continued to howl. Farmers, with the encouragement of the United States government, had plowed more and more land to provide wheat for world markets. Now, the dry land itself lifted and blew east in great rolling black clouds of dust. Beth-El General Hospital was perched precariously on the western edge of the Great American Dust Bowl.[71] As the drought rolled on year after year, and the depression deepened, hope for the future was difficult to sustain.

Mr. Guy Hanner redoubled his efforts of fundraising. He also took a very "hands on" approach to the conduct of education and hospital budgets, school matters, and student activities. Miss Mary Kay Smith, who came to Beth-El as an instructor in 1930, quickly became the Director of Nurses and the School of Nursing. She was a steadfast leader and talented nurse educator who seemed to be everywhere at once. Students fondly remembered her as strict but always fair in her decisions. Arleen Prentice Campbell, class of 1942, fondly remembered, "She expected great things of Beth-El students."[72] Her professional standards echoed those of Florence Standish, 20 years earlier. Beth-El nurses continued their reputation of giving excellent nursing care. Even as resources dwindled, and people needed care more than ever, student nurses carefully used, cleaned, and patched worn hospital supplies and equipment. Miss Smith encouraged them to "improvise." Hospitals could not afford to hire nurses, so students worked even longer hours, although there were many graduate nurses who desperately needed work to support themselves and their families. The hospital depended more heavily on gifts of canned vegetables, fruits, eggs, and donations of every kind from churches on Colorado's western slope. Students remembered the patients received the best food while the students sometimes ate bitter fruit canned with a bare minimum of sugar.

Throughout the years, visitors from the Colorado State Board of Nurse Examiners made thorough visits to assess all aspects of the students' education and hospital environment. No aspect escaped their notice. They commented on the untold number of hours students spent in the hospital kitchen setting up meals then serving the trays. All levels of students spent excessive hours staffing the sanatorium and hospital during evening and night hours. It was clear to the Examiners: the whole operation was just managing to remain viable. Their greatest concern was the inordinate control the administrator exerted over the school and student admissions. They saw it was difficult to retain a stable faculty and experienced nursing staff with limited support and a poor educational environment. They also observed inconsistent educational follow-up and support for the students. These observations and recommendations exerted a major influence on the hospital administration. State Board accreditation was mandatory to remain open no matter how much a community valued a hospital and school of nursing.[73] The Colorado State Board Examiners assessed all nursing schools with the same keen eye. Schools that did not receive accreditation closed. Beth-El received transfer students from several Colorado community hospitals.[74]

National and local events did not noticeably affect the students' lives; they focused on daily classes, assignments, duty hours, and patient care. Everyone worked hard and made do with what was available without whining (much). The students brought comfort with their thoughtful and concerned care. They soothed and heartened patients who felt the anxiety and stress of the hard times, along with sharing the joy of birth, or fear of illness, and death.

Mildred Kane Woolley, a class of 1942 graduate, clearly remembered morning chapel services in the hospital parlor.

> Those of us going on duty were required to meet for [6:30 am] chapel. We sang beautiful hymns; most of us were Protestant and familiar with the hymns. We sang the parts, alto, and soprano. The patients loved hearing us as we sang. At some point, that practice ceased, and many patients expressed that they missed having us sing. When we left chapel we had an inspection by Mary Kay Smith; no

rolled hose, hairnets required under caps. We wore white hose and during those war years, all hosiery was scarce. We always had a needle and white thread so we could repair any runners.[75]

Hospital Parlor

The parlor where students had morning Chapel. Patients asked to have their doors opened so they could hear the students singing hymns.

Another student in the class of 1942, Arleen Prentice Campbell, recalled student activities held in Daniels Hall, located between the hospital and nurses home.

Of course, there was the library and study hall, [also] square dancing, folk dancing, parties, social functions, basketball, and rehabilitation for the Crippled Children.[76]

Classmate, Esther Green Hill added,

> We were not allowed to be married throughout our schooling.[77]

Medical treatments ordered for patients remained much as they had been in earlier years. The 1935 Beth-El Procedure Manual held complete instructions for necessary nursing procedures such as mustard plasters (also called sinapisms), turpentine stupes, and eight different types of enemas. Morning and evening comfort care known as "ablutions" included a full bed bath in the morning. Patients received a partial bath as needed in the evening, with mouth care and a back rub (for a period, a Swedish masseuse taught proper massage technique). As a final touch, sheets were tightened or changed if needed. The procedure read regarding care, "To be passed to every patient at seven a.m. and after four o'clock in the afternoon."[78]

The Colorado Springs community continued doing what they could to support services at Beth-El General Hospital. Mr. Hanner was an active leader in both the Shriners and Rotary Clubs. He enlisted the help of the Shriners to establish a children's ward for crippled children. In 1934, the Rotary Clubs of the Seventh District joined in the support of the Crippled Children's Ward. The Rotarians also furnished rooms and sponsored children's treatment. Physician members often provided services free of charge. Dr. E. L. Timmons and Dr. George Bancroft provided care for hundreds of infants and young children for little or no charge. Mr. and Mrs. C. W. Daniels of Pueblo built a Crippled Children's Recreation Hall, known as Daniels Hall in 1937. Mr. Daniels was a Rotarian and Mrs. Daniels a member of the local

Woman's Board.[79]

December 7, 1941—suddenly, the nation was at war (World War II)! Life changed at that moment and yet the routine for students remained oddly the same. The "boys" needed registered nurses "over there" as well as nurses for folks at home. As nurses went off to war, additional senior nursing students moved into head nurse positions. Students joined the Cadet Nurse Corps in 1943, with a pledge to serve where needed in the military or civilian agencies for the duration of the war and six months after that. Daniels Hall became the dorm for the Cadet Nurses.[80]

Rationing became the norm for all materials and supplies. Student uniforms were restyled to a simple one-piece uniform of blue fabric for freshman and white for junior and senior students; both uniforms had white collar and cuffs.[81]

During these tumultuous years, administration and maintenance of Beth-El General Hospital and School of Nursing became more difficult for the National Board of Hospitals and Homes of the Methodist Episcopal Church. Beth-El was the last hospital they owned, and they wished to move on to other services. Two or three other parties indicated interest in purchasing the operation, which sparked animated community conversations.[82]

On January 12, 1942, in anticipation of the impending sale, the local Women's Board of Beth-El formally dissolved to become charter members of a new organization called White Cross Mother Guild of Beth-El Hospital. This group met monthly to sew for the American Red Cross and to support the Nurses Home and Beth-El Hospital. Ten additional churches in Colorado Springs also formed White Cross Guilds in continued support of their hospital and made bandages for the war effort.[83]

1942 Nursing Rounds

Students and their instructor on "nursing care rounds" at a patient's bedside. The uniforms worn by the students reflect the simpler one-piece uniforms adopted during the strict rationing enacted during World War II.

[59] Opel Stanford Rutherford, interview by Jean John, director, Beth-El School of Nursing, Colorado Springs, 1986.

[60] "First Unit National Methodist Sanatorium to be Opened to Patients on Next Friday," *Colorado Springs Gazette*, Section D 1–8, August 8, 1926; E. L. Mosley, "Interim report on Bethel Hospital and the National Methodist Sanitarium" January 19, 1943, Beth-El Alumni Collection, UCCS Archives.

[61] Beth-El Yearbook Committee, *TPR* Beth-El Yearbook (Colorado Springs: Beth-El School of Nursing, 1930), 67.

[62] Irene Neese Hall, "Beth-El Alumni Questionnaire" Binder 1932, Beth-El Alumni Collection, UCCS Archives.

[63] Joanne F. Ruth, *Beth-El Alumni Newsletter*, 1993.

[64] "The Beth-El Hospital Bulletin," December 1929, 7.

[65] "The Beth-El Hospital Bulletin," December 1929, 7

[66] Dorothy Hamilton Burkhart, "Beth-El Alumni Questionnaire" and letter, Binder 1938, Beth-El Alumni Collection, UCCS Archives.

[67] *Report of Beth-El School of Nursing Visit* (Denver: Colorado State Board of Nurse Examiners, 1931).

[68] Goldmark, *Nursing and Nursing Education in the United States*, 1923, reprint 1984, 7 – 30.

[69] Beth-El Yearbook Committee, *TPR* Beth-El Yearbook (Colorado Springs: Beth-El School of Nursing, 1926), 22.

[70] M. Patricia Donahue, *Nursing the Finest Art: An Illustrated History* (Saint Louis: The C.V. Mosby Company, 1985), 382–387.

[71] Timothy Egan, *The Worst Hard Time: The Untold Story of Those Who Survived the Great American Dust Bowl* (New York: Houghton Mifflin Co., 2006).

[72] Arleene Prentice Campbell, "Beth-El Alumni Questionnaire" Binder 1942, Beth-El Alumni Collection, UCCS Archives.

[73] *Report of Beth-El School of Nursing Visit* (Denver: Colorado State Board of Nurse Examiners, 1929–1931).

[74] Marie Robb Thornton, "Beth-El Alumni Questionnaire" Binder 1935, Beth-El Alumni Collection, UCCS.

[75] Mildred Kane Woolley, Letter, May 2014, Binder 1942, Beth-El Alumni Collection, UCCS Archives.

[76] Campbell, "Beth-El Alumni Questionnaire," 1942.

[77] Esther Green Hill, *Beth-El Chart Yearbook*, 1992, 14.

[78] Beth-El Hospital, *Procedure Manual Beth-El Hospital* (Colorado Springs, 1935), 34.

[79] Smith, "Beth-El Woman's Board Yesterday and Today," 9, 10, 11.

[80] Dorothy Schwab Vosler, "Beth-El Alumni Questionnaire" Binder 1946, Beth-El Alumni Collection, UCCS Archives.

[81] Philip A. Kalisch and Beatrice J Kalisch, *The Changing Image of the Nurse* (Menlo Park: Addison-Wesley, 1987), 101; "Student Nurse Officers," *Colorado Springs Gazette*, December 1, 1948.

[82] Smith, "Beth-El Woman's Board Yesterday and Today," 13.

[83] Smith, "Beth-El Woman's Board Yesterday and Today," 12.

The Photo Gallery

1926 Beth-El Alumnae Association Formal Portrait
Above is the photo from the 1926 yearbook, which is also on the front cover of this book. Julia Ray Work is in the middle row, second from left.

Julia Ray Work
Class of 1913

73

1904 Deaconess Hospital

In 1911, the building changed to a home for ill "colored pastors." It was sold to the Colorado School for the Deaf and Blind in 1917. Later, it transferred to the Sisters of St. Francis for a nurses residence until it was later torn down.

c1912 A Lighthearted Moment for the Camera

Julia Ray Work, second in line, poses with some of her classmates during a break in their day of hard work.

1909 Beth-El Hospital, Unfinished

The thick brick, fire proof walls were left unfiinished when funds ran out in 1909.

1923 View of Beth-El Hospital

Taken from the Nurses Home looking West beyond Beth-El Hospital, is the ever-present Pikes Peak.

"Airplane view of Beth-El General Hospital and Sanatorium"

Beth-El Hospital

Three features of the hospital are indicated with shapes. Compare them to the picture below to find where the original hospital is enclosed in the new structure. The feet of the star stand on the same ledge in both photos.

1984 Looking South from the South Patient Tower

While the top photo is from the front, this view is from behind, looking down on the hospital and across the street. Compare the symbols to find where the old building is.

**1915 Florence E Standish's
Nob Hill Lodge Sanatorium**

Looking southeast from Beth-El are the Gardiner "tents" and associated Lodge buildings, center left. Idlewold Sanatorium, owned by Lois Shardlow (right of center) is still standing. Union Printers Home is in the far distance.

Nob Hill Lodge

Nob Hill's main building was later used as a faculty home in 1931. It remains on Logan Avenue south of the hospital.

1920 Student Nurses Room
Students' room in the new nurses residence.

1920 Living Room of Nurses Home
The students gathered in their living room to sing together around the piano, play games, and to just relax after long shifts and grueling lectures and study.

1926 Christmas for the Students

Three students pose by the Nurses Home Christmas tree in about the year 1926.

1925 Beth-El Basketball Team

The black wool uniforms featured fashionable middy collars trimmed in white, and knee-length black bloomers.

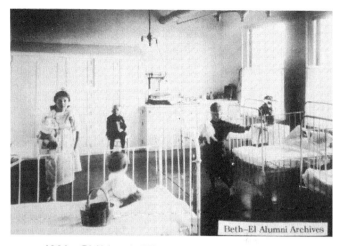

1920s Children's Ward, first floor east wing
Pediatric patients stop for a moment to pose for the camera in the bright sunlight streaming in their windows.

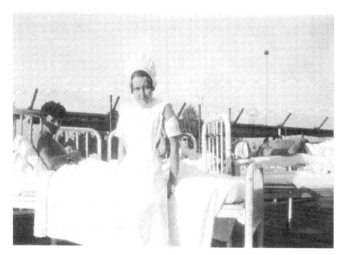

1931 Sanatorium Open Air and Sun Therapy
Evangeline Deyo, class of 1931, poses with her patients, young men in beds taking their daily prescribed sunbaths on the "San" roof.

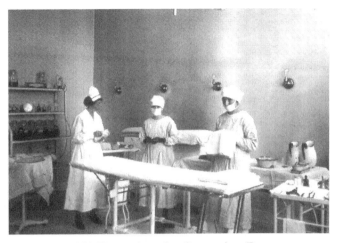

1920 Preparing the Operating Room
A supervisor helps student nurses prepare the OR to
receive a patient for surgery.

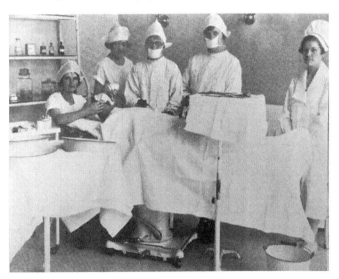

1927 A Patient and OR Team
Ether is delivered by the sitting nurse at the head of the
patient as the supervisor stands at the foot of the table.

1920 Special Diet Kitchen

Students worked many hours learning how to prepare nutritious meals and snacks in this kitchen.

1928 Patients and a Student Nurse on the "San" Roof

To benefit from open air and sun therapy, patients are moved to beds on the porch of the sanatorium.

1913 Children at the Children's Pavilion

The Pavilion was funded by the VNA and Beth-El Hospital. The children slept in open sleeping porches and spent most of the waking hours in the fresh air. Here, they brush their teeth together on their open air porch.

1928 Nutrition Camp: Children Exercising for Health

All activities and classes were held outside to provide the maximum exposure to the sun and fresh air.

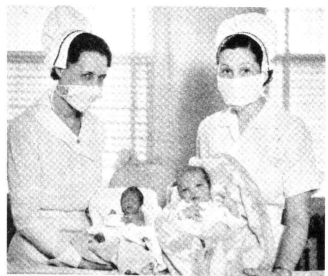

1936 Two Beth-El Babies Born 24 Hours Apart

Nursing supervisor Irene Neece Hall, class of 1932, holds a 2 ¾ pound baby next to a baby just shy of 10 pounds, held by Dorothea Close Farmer, class of 1936.

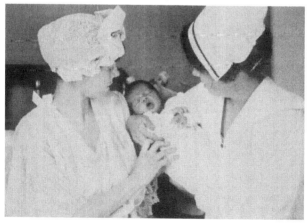

1916 "Mary Stewart's Last Baby Case"

Mary Stewart, class of 1916, shared a caring moment with a mom and her sleeping newborn baby.

Our Hospital

Between broad walls of white and gray
Are the homey rooms where the patients stay.
The little red bells hang down from the wall;
That the feeble and sick might their willing nurse call.
There is a shaded door way still,
But a happy hope has crossed the sill.

There is the O. R. and, as of yore;
I can smell the ether from the open door.
And, see the nurses all so busy there;
Also hear the doctors whispered prayer.
But the patient's come—Oh! aching pain;
His bones to mend or an abscess to drain.

There's the D. R. where babies are born.
Where courageous mothers are tired and worn;
And their children grow up and go out in the world
To gain success, or in pain be hurled.
Starting from the nursery and thru old age,
Somebody suffers to the end of the page.

Oh ye who weekly pay your bill;
Give generously! for you're with us still.
And, when you think of that poor broken soul;
Aren't you happier because of the pain you've eased while
reaching your goal

Deal kindly with these tired souls;
And when the year around you rolls
You can say from the very start;
As if old memories stirred your heart,
I have helped to lighten the load,
And also scattered sunshine along the road.

—S. LAMPRECHT.

Our Hospital

A poem written by Sylvia (Sally) Lamprecht Boggs, class of
1931, for the 1931 *TPR* Beth-El yearbook.

c1953 New Front Entrance to the Hospital
Students wear navy blue, gold-lined capes.

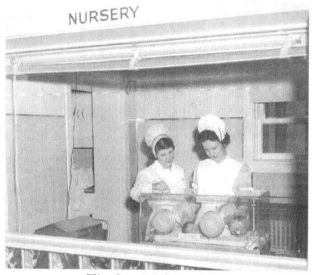

The Special Care Nursery
A Beth-El graduate and Junior nursing student attend a premature newborn in an Isolette in the nursery.

Beth-El Student with Her Instructor

The student demonstrates the skill and art of preparing medications and filling a syringe.

1962 Student Room

Two nursing students enjoy their newly remodeled student room in the Nurses Home.

1996 Master of Science in Nursing Graduates

Graduation was held at the First United Methodist Church of Colorado Springs.

1996 Alumni Homecoming

Eight alumni gather for their annual Beth-El Homecoming with Dean Carole Schoffstall (right) on the campus of Beth-El College of Nursing and Health Sciences at the Offices at the Park.

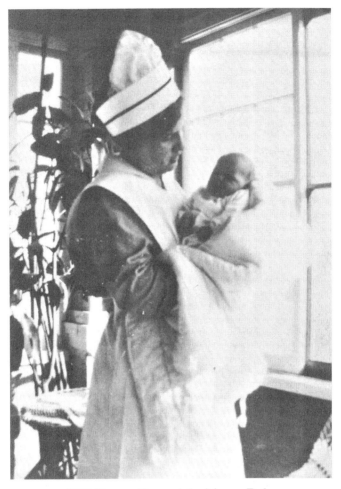

1926 Emma Brace Admiring a Baby
On a sun porch of Beth-El Hospital, this picture and the following photo were the featured theme images in the Eightieth Anniversary exhibit at the Pioneers Museum in 1984.

1981 Donna Modisett Stewart Admiring a Baby

Beth-El student Donna Modisett Stewart, class of 1981, holds a baby, recreating the Brace photo seen on page 90. The similarities between the photos were noticed only after the photo was published. The reflective windows of the new south tower of Memorial Hospital are in the background.

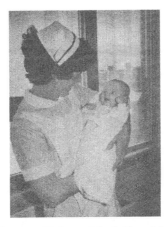

1983 Tammy Palmer Modeling New Cap

Class President Tammy Palmer, class of 1984, displays the new cap she designed, which was adopted by Beth-El.

2004 Evolution of the Beth-El Uniforms

Beth-El students wore the uniforms of their predecessors and their current uniforms at the Gala Dinner celebrating the Centennial Year of Beth-El College of Nursing and Health Sciences.

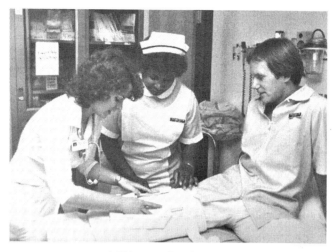

A Diverse Institution

From its initial makeup of only Caucasian women, Beth-El has grown into a diverse institution with a student body comprised of women *and* men, and people of many creeds and diverse ethnic and racial backgrounds. The first two African Americans graduated in 1953 and the first male students graduated in 1966. Above, Cass Fox Wood R.N., class of 1979, employee of Memorial Hospital, demonstrates how to utilize and secure a leg brace for students Caroline Ford and Robert Schulz, both class of 1984.

JOANNE RUTH

Memorial Hospital and Beth-El School of Nursing

1400 East Boulder

1922–1943

Beth-El General Hospital 1933 Commemorative Pen and Ink Drawing

This drawing was created by a talented, unknown patient of the sanatorium for Lydia Dazey Hornbeck's class of 1933 handmade and unpublished yearbook. In 1984, Mrs. Hornbeck gave permission to have the drawing reproduced as a celebratory memento of Beth-El School of Nursing. (The 12"x 15" drawing is suitable for framing and is available through the UCCS Archives, Kraemer Family Library Office.[84])

February 9, 1943. Colorado Springs City Council voted five to three to buy the one hundred twenty-five bed Beth-El General Hospital for $76,500, or a half of the hospital's indebtedness. There were two additional offers for the hospital pending, one from the Mennonites, and another from an unnamed party.[85]

January 19, 1943. Mr. E. L. Mosley, City Manager of Colorado Springs, wrote an "interim report on Bethel Hospital and the National Methodist Sanatorium for the Mayor [Ralph J. Gilmore] and Members of the Colorado Springs City Council." In the report, he described the several buildings that housed a range of valuable health care services, detailed hospital activities, identified community affiliations, finances, and operating statements. He attached a sketch or plat of the hospital property and location of all buildings associated with Beth-El General Hospital, School of Nursing, and the National Methodist Sanatorium.[86]

The city renamed the hospital "Memorial Hospital," in honor of the men and women who lost their lives in World War II. The hospital began operating as a municipal facility on June 1, 1943. Beth-El School of Nursing elected to maintain their traditional name. Almost immediately, the city transferred the former National Methodist Sanatorium and its 20 acres to the Army Air Force for what would become Ent Air Force Base and Headquarters for the 15th Air Force.[87] Colorado Springs transferred the land and buildings to the Olympic Training Center in 1977.[88]

Plat Showing Property Owned by
BETHEL HOSPITAL January 1943 [89]

The plat provides a visual foundation of the historical development of BETHEL as well as a visual platform from which to place future buildings and services created by succeeding generations of dedicated community-minded citizens.

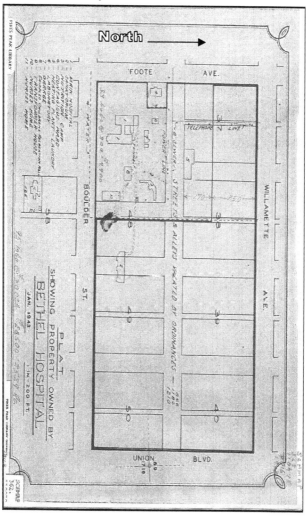

97

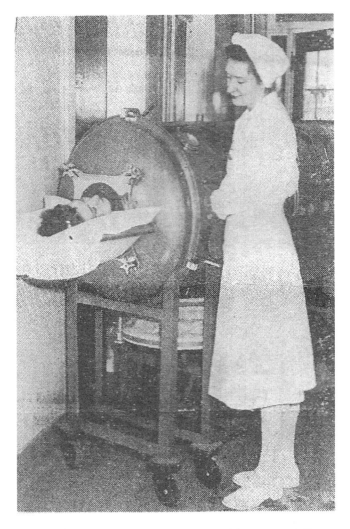

"A patient in an 'Iron Lung' and her nurse." [90]
Memorial Hospital owned three "iron lungs" that helped save many lives during the long years of the polio epidemic.

In August 1944, when the polio epidemic arrived in Colorado Springs, Beth-El nurses and students accepted responsibility for the care of children and adults in the former Observation Hospital, commonly known as Contagion Hospital. The Sister Kenny Hot Pack Treatment seemed the most effective treatment. Mable Meyer Bishop, class of 1946, reminisced:

> I remember so well the work that was involved. There was an old ringer washing machine and wool pieces of material for legs, arms, and backs. You would wring them out, put them in plastic wrap, and put them on the patient. Leave them on the prescribed time and then remove and start all over again.[91]

There was only one night nurse, recalled Lorene Ellis Hall, class of 1944, when interviewed.

Beth-El faculty and medical colleagues offered a four-day intensive workshop for professionals interested in enhancing their comprehensive knowledge of polio patients. There were topics on pathology, treatment modalities, acute nursing care, as well as rehabilitation and Public Health aspects of patients with poliomyelitis for a community sorely tested by fear and pain in 1947.[92]

Memorial Hospital Annex
427 North Foote Avenue

Memorial Annex [93]

This simple, unimposing building provided essential space for the care of individuals with contagious diseases just as it had for the previous 30 years. Students and nurses maintained strict isolation technique. If a student contracted any one of several communicable diseases, the event would have been considered a basis for dismissal because the student had "broken technique."

Memorial Hospital experienced a "hospitalization boom" in 1947 and desperately required more beds. On January 1, 1948, El Paso County transferred their stake in Observation Hospital to the city, which added 36 beds available for medical patients.[94] Unfortunately, as more beds opened up, apparently the hospital did not hire enough registered nurses to provide an adequate number of supervisors—much less graduate nurses—for each shift. Patricia Anne Jacobs, class of 1948, remembered:

> There was only one graduate on duty many times, and a hospital full of

student nurses trying to do things we were unprepared for.... We students worked eleven to seven and three to eleven, so we would be off for classes.... New mothers stayed in bed five days, and in the hospital ten; abdominal surgery [stayed] about the same [time]. I had an appendectomy summer of 1948, done by Dr. Louis Kennedy, who had recently come back from the army, and he got me out of bed the same evening. Big change! We used mustard plasters [for chest congestion and distention] and alcohol baths for elevated temperatures. [We] did not wear gloves for sterile procedures such as catheterization, but scrubbed [our hands and lower arms] for ten minutes. We resterilized rubber intravenous tubing and patched surgical gloves.[95]

Students and nurses commonly shared many of these straightforward experiences during the previous years. There were several societal and local impacts on the provision of care. Following the war years, it took some time to recover from the shortages of rubber, metal, cloth material, and medications. However, there was an even more acute concern of maintaining stable leadership of hospital administration, nursing service, and nursing education directors.

The City Council struggled with establishing city funding strategies. Before the purchase of Beth-El General Hospital, they had little knowledge of hospital and nursing school requirements, responsibilities, and funding. The City Council also may have had only partial understanding of the depth of broad commitment and philanthropic dedication maintained by citizens during the previous 50 years. They struggled to open and maintain the hospital and school of nursing, of which they were justly proud.

Another longstanding and complex national issue threaded its way through the conflict. That was the question of what was the best way to educate nursing students. If student nurses were not available to do the required nursing care in the hospital, could a hospital afford to hire graduate nurses and auxiliary staff to replace them? What impact would this have on the availability of nurses in Colorado Springs? Again, the community was asking, will we have nurses? Another concern entered the conversation. The purpose of educational institutions such as a school of nursing was to educate nurses; however, was the hospital environment, by itself, optimal for education?

The National League of Nursing Education published *A Curriculum Guide for School of Nursing* by Isabel Stewart in 1937. As the premier national nursing curriculum expert, Miss Stewart also wrote *The Education of Nurses* in 1943. (These two outstanding works provided significant facts, and the insight that demonstrated relationships of knowledge and care.) They also provided a philosophy for the curriculum and a guide for professional nursing education. These works and others provided the basic philosophy from which the National League of Nursing Education developed educational recommendations and standards. The American Nurses Association also studied educational concerns and published position papers that expanded professional and public recognition of these visions for the future of nursing.[96]

Local community conversations exploded when in 1949, Colorado Springs City Council voted to close Beth-El School of Nursing. Reports in the *Gazette* followed the heated discussions and protests from citizens, doctors, dentists, and Beth-El Alumni. They identified the limited and reluctant support previously given to the School of Nursing and Hospital.[97] There were many additional articles published at the time.

The people of the city had struggled to build the hospital and continued to staunchly supported "their" school of nursing. The question of support went forward to voters with a referendum held September 22, 1949. Voters formally approved to continue city operation of the hospital and school of nursing 3,235 to 1,479. A $400,000 bond issue included $7,000 for new furnishings for the School of Nursing/Junior Nurses Home.

Nineteen rooms in the residence received new modern metal furnishings; the Nursing Arts Laboratory received Simmons beds, bedside and over-bed tables, and bedside chairs. A sterilizer and a charting desk similar to those used in hospital wards were a welcome addition.[98] The largest portion of the bond issue established a Board of Trustees and authorized a three-story addition, known as the "Sunshine Wing" or simply, West Wing. On June 19, 1952, the first two floors opened with the latest patient care improvements in the new construction. The architects designed a ground level front entrance, which removed the original steps up to the second floor.[99] (See close-up of new entrance on page 87.)

*Memorial Hospital Entrance
and West Wing*

A new entrance with circular driveway and landscaping provided a modern appearance as well as a readily accessible entry. The original stately stairs and formal doorway into the second floor of the structure were gone; however, the entry columns and cornerstone remained in place. Photo by Stewarts Commercial Photographers.

Grace Bodenstein Heath, class of 1946, wrote a celebratory front-page article for the *Beth-El Alumni Newsletter*, October, 1949.

HEAR YE! HEAR YE! VICTORY FOR BETH-EL!!!

Have you heard that YOUR Hospital and Training School have been fighting for their lives during the last few years? Do you know that YOUR Alumnae Association, 97 doctors and dentists, the present administrative, teaching staff and students, along with many friends, carried on an intensive campaign to keep the hospital and school? So much pressure was brought to the City Council that a special city election was held last month to settle the problem. At this election, the voters decided that the hospital should be retained by the city, and the training school should be continued. Alumnae's future goals included assisting with student recruitment, financial assistance to students nurses through an active loan fund, and service to the training school. In the past, they had "helped with [the] redecoration of the Nurses Home, bought a new Chase doll [nursing practice model], a 16mm movie projector, and a radio-phonograph console for the nurses lounge."[100]

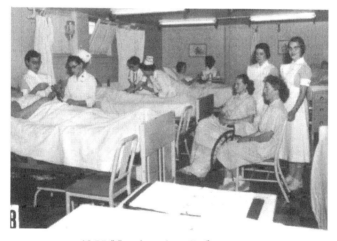

c1955 Nursing Arts Laboratory
Instructor Ruth Gaston R.N. (second from left) assists students with clinical skills practice in the sparkling new Nursing Arts Laboratory located in the basement of the Nurses Home basement.

Alice McAdams Morgan was the first African-American student admitted to Beth-El School of Nursing in 1950. Sadly, segregation had been a cultural norm in the city. Alice experienced many hurtful and unfortunate difficulties. Another African-

American student, Eglantine Wilson Payne, enrolled later, and all 12 classmates proudly graduated September 4, 1953.[101] Both women had highly distinguished nursing careers.

Through the years, Beth-El had worked diligently to establish high quality basic physical and social science courses; however, each plan fell short for a range of reasons. The Beth-El alumnae remembered a variety of arrangements with classes offered by Colorado College, on their campus and at Beth-El. They also contracted with Colorado College to offer basic social science courses. The Colorado University at Colorado Springs Extension taught science courses at Beth-El for a short time in the early 1950s. Beth-El hired faculty to teach basic sciences courses for a few years, though it was difficult to maintain continuity and quality. From 1956–1964, students attended Colorado College for all college courses. The University of Colorado at Colorado Springs opened on September 20, 1965. The first two floors of Cragmor Hall (Main Hall) and Cragmor Manor classrooms and offices were almost ready for students and faculty.[102] Beth-El students were among the first on campus. Students were required to wear uniforms to classes and rode the Memorial Hospital bus to the university.

Carol Gibson Grimm, class of 1955, reflected on student leadership responsibilities of the patient care, standard health care, and hospital practices of the 1950s:

> As students, we were in charge of entire floors, usually covering the "whole house" three to eleven and eleven to seven, with [only] one house supervisor. Students were

doing all Rx, [treatments] and starting IVs [intravenous lines]. [We were] learning pride of nursing and [hoped to] never again be asked to be [nurses' aides] or work as nurses' aides. Students [worked] in the delivery room, doing exams [and] helping in Delivery. *Responsibility!* Students who lived and breathed nursing for three years, lost [their] former identity and [could] no longer remember being anything but a nurse.[103]

Wanda Bauder, class of 1958, also remembered usual practices of the time:

We helped sharpen needles and sterilized them. We used glass syringes, which we had to wrap in cloth and sterilize. We washed, dried, and powdered gloves before sterilizing. At this time, everything had to be sterilized in Central Supply. On the floors, we used metal bedpans that were cleaned and sterilized in a hopper; water was a must [on] each shift and pitchers were washed on the night shift. Mr. Fielden (Executive Director) had a good idea to decrease kitchen help if employees on the floors would run dishes on floors, so he installed dishwashers on each floor. This [plan] did not go over very well! Back rubs were a must at bedtime and after morning baths. Hot moist towels were used for thrombophlebitis of extremities (much fun trying to keep them hot but not burn the patient).[104]

Students continued to expand educational and hospital experiences with three-month clinical experiences at Children's Hospital (1921–1963). They also spent four to six months at National Jewish Hospital (1954–c1960) for the study of tuberculosis and problems of the chest. Psychiatric nursing experience at Colorado State Hospital in Pueblo varied through the years from three months to nine weeks. Public health nursing experience at the El Paso County Department of Health varied from year to year.

Memorial Hospital closed Idlewold as the senior dorm in 1951. The administration remodeled the home for the Executive Director, Mr. C. Franklin Fielden. This decision, of course, displaced the students. They moved back into the Nurses Home on Boulder Street for a couple of years until Mr. Fielden identified their next home. The hospital administration decided to convert the all-purpose building, known as the Memorial Annex, from "mothballs" to a dormitory for the students. The building was originally Observation Hospital, built in 1918.

Senior Beth-El Hall
427 North Foote Avenue
1953–1973

This building was convenient and available, but it was a much less homey accommodation. Hospital maintenance men scrubbed, painted, and "fixed-up" the 1918 building in preparation for its new purpose. However, they did not remove the laundry chute and dumb-waiter, and of course, students gleefully pushed the buttons as the dumb-waiter rumbled, creaked, and rose from the basement to the second floor. Myths and ghost stories seemed to come from the walls into imaginative student conversations. As the years wore on, even the history of this building was lost to the current student residents. No matter what happened, students continued to work long hours caring for Colorado Springs and statewide residents, studying for "State Boards" and building lifelong relationships.

The first schools of nursing for men in the United States, "Mills School for Nursing and St. Vincent's Hospital School for Men were founded in New York in 1888. The Pennsylvania Hospital opened a school for female nurses in 1914 and simultaneously opened a separate men's nursing school."[105] In 1966, the first male students graduated from Beth-El; they were Neil Milar and Lotar Semmler. Neil was the first active duty military person to graduate from Beth-El and return to duty as a licensed nurse.[106] This local milestone signified a subtle but important change for the Beth-El Alumnae Association. They were now properly known as The Beth-El Alumni Association.

Senior students of 1968 class thoughtfully remembered their junior year in the 1968 yearbook:

> Although the Nursing curriculum is very full, there was time to think of others. Projects were established to fulfill many goals. First, it provided an outlet whereby we could release our abilities in avenues, which were like, yet unlike, our nursing course. Secondly, we were able to employ various methods of communications. Thirdly, it opened our eyes further to see a

need in our own community. Fourthly, the community was able to observe how we, as a unit, could work together effectively. Projects included entertainment for the patients [on the ward were they worked] in Central Division at the Colorado State Mental Hospital. Patients looked forward to the program and responded positively. One comment, which was overheard [by the students] during a particular comical number, was to the effect, "they're crazier than we are!" "Happiness is sharing" was our theme in two Christmas programs to Nursing Homes.... Over 50 children from the Deaf and Blind school were dressed in costumes and taken trick or treating. Their excitement and enthusiasm will never be forgotten.[107]

A hard-fought city election held on April 6, 1971, again asked voters to decide whether to keep Beth-El School of Nursing open. The alumni vigorously brought to the public attention the value of the school. To the surprise of the City Council, the voters supported the referendum by more than two to one margin (9,679 to 4,652). The question won in all precincts of the city.[108]

On April 4, 1973, voters approved a $15 million bond issue to add a seven-floor wing for patient rooms, with a three to one margin. The plans stated that the south patient tower was to be located where the Observation Hospital (then housing the School of Nursing) stood, expanding the number of beds to 300. The money raised also went to expanding services and providing for a two-story parking garage on the former site of Nurses Home. Beth-El School of Nursing began a long odyssey of moving from one place to next place as hospital expansion marched forward. At the end of five years, the school would have moved four times.[109]

Simultaneously, nursing education was changing. Diploma schools across the country were moving to offer a two-year Associate Degree in Nursing (ADN) program, or to step forward to a four-year Baccalaureate (BSN) degree. It seemed clear; the only other alternative was to close the school completely. No matter which path the school would ultimately follow, faculty members recognized the imperative to extend their educational preparation to include a Master of Science in Nursing (MSN). As Beth-El moved from one place to the next, the faculty continued their advanced educational endeavors to be ready for the future, whatever it held.

"Beth-El on The Move"
Four Locations in Five Years

Beth-El School of Nursing moved from the original Nurses Home on Boulder Street over to the former Beth-El Senior Dorm at 427 North Foote Avenue in 1973. After this point, Beth-El School of Nursing no longer operated dormitories for students. There was a deep sense of loss which prevailed in the collective identity and common purpose of the student body. Memorial Hospital demolished the Nurses Home and Daniels Hall in the summer of 1974 in preparation for building a two-story parking structure. At the same time, Beth-El faculty and students prepared to make way for construction of a seven-story patient tower planned for the 427 North Foote Avenue site. This location was across the alley, north of the Memorial Hospital West Wing addition.[110]

The next destination, in late summer of 1974, was 1721 East Dale Street, the former Ent Air Force Base Building 87. This was a large three-story building that had been a dormitory for airmen. In an odd way, students felt "at home," as library books and nursing arts lab equipment arrived in the building. A 1968 map of Ent Air Force Base illustrated all buildings on the base, to include Building 87 and Building 48 (the next temporary home for the school). Base Headquarters was located in the former National Methodist Sanatorium building situated on Boulder Street.[111] (See Airplane View, page 76.)

In 1975, the city, in a bid to enhance business and national prestige, transferred the total property of the former Ent Air Force Base to the United States Olympic Committee for future development of a high-altitude training center. "Our" building was to become an Olympic athlete dormitory.[112]

Even though uncertainty abounded, students and faculty continued work toward future academic goals. Jean Johns, Director, joyfully reported to the alumni in April 1976:

> One of our greatest thrills was the awarding of a $10,000 Capitation Grant from the United States Department of Health, Education and Welfare (HEW) to be spent on BSN [Beth-El School of Nursing] merger plans, the library and visual aids. [Also,] the Helene Fuld Trust Fund provided a $30,000 grant providing us with $5,000 in new library books, a closed circuit

television system, and six fully equipped
student carrels. National League for Nursing
and State Board of Nurse Examiners both
made accreditation visits in October 1975. It
has all paid off as we now have the
maximum six-year accreditation from NLN
(through 1981) and the three-year maximum
accreditation from State Board.[113]

The population of male students had grown to
ten percent of the student body. Graduates were
doing well on State Board examinations for registered
nurse licensure. Alumni continued to hold enviable
reputations as outstanding nurses throughout the
country.

In 1976, Beth-El School of Nursing again packed
up for the next move to temporary quarters in an old
wooden Ent Air Force Base Building 48, located at
the corner of Foote Avenue and Willamette Avenue.
Unfortunately, the hospital tower and hospital
remodeling, with the promise of a future location in
the hospital itself, would not be complete for two
more years. The new setting was very "cozy" with
only two classrooms, a nursing arts lab, space for a
small library and student lounge, and very small
faculty offices. However, being closer to the hospital
was an advantage, and there was an outdoor
courtyard. Exploration of future opportunities to
offer a BSN continued. There were many complex
aspects considered and obstacles to overcome, along
with new opportunities to explore.[114]

Cheers abounded for Memorial Hospital on July
7, 1977. Mr. J. Robert Peters, Executive Director of
the hospital, wrote in the *Beth-El Alumni Newsletter*,
"The new seven-story patient tower was dedicated to

the acclaim of more than 5,000 community supporters who toured the facility. Remodeling on the old hospital building is underway, and is expected to be completed this summer. We now have 146 beds and when remodeling is complete will go to 206 beds."[115]

Mrs. Johns announced that the largest graduation group of 33 seniors would graduate May 26, 1978. Demographic data of the student body had dramatically changed with 50 percent married; the average age of freshman was 25 years. Also noted was the fact that all members of the faculty held a master's degree and three of them were working on doctoral degrees. Faculty and students excitedly made plans for a late summer move to newly renovated school space in the southeast wing, third floor of the original hospital building. Yes, the double brick fireproof walls throughout the hospital were still in place, just as it had been built in 1912. The whole building, encased in a new brick wraparound, provided a uniform front appearance. Classrooms filled the former front courtyard space between the two wings. The students and faculty had demonstrated flexibility, perseverance, and dedication to nursing education excellence during the previous five years. Foremost was the faculty's vision and determination to offer a Bachelor of Science in Nursing degree for eager students and residents of the Pikes Peak region.[116]

At last, over 1978 "Christmas break" the faculty moved the school into Memorial Hospital, 1400 East Boulder Street, east wing, south half of the third floor. This space had welcomed mothers and new infants during the previous 60 years. Now, students and faculty were "home." At least that is what everyone thought or hoped at the time.

Students took a deep breath, enjoyed new classrooms, a nursing arts lab, offices, and a floor that did not bounce one bit when they walked down the hall. There had been no time to take stock of the odyssey they had traveled during the previous six years. In the fall of 1981, the yearbook staff decided to celebrate the history of the school in the 1982 yearbook. With dismay, they discovered the school office had no historical information about the school. The hospital had only one small folder related to hospital history.

The faculty and students had been focused on pressing academic activity and preparing for tomorrow; there had been little time or energy to recognize, value, or document past experiences. Beth-El's Seventy-fifth Anniversary had come and gone in 1979 without awareness. The alumni, of course, had keen memories of their years in school; it seemed "it was only yesterday." As they related their stories, it quickly became apparent Beth-El was a part of a long-standing and complex community endeavor. The students and alumni alike were eager to discover deeper details of their student experiences.

It was at this juncture that I, Jo Ruth, member of the Beth-El School of Nursing faculty, joined the narrative of this story. As faculty advisor for the yearbook, the *Beth-El Chart*, I with the students, valued the history of the school and wanted to document the Beth-El legacy. In order to collect and preserve the memories regarding the hospital and school of the alumni nurses, I developed a four-page questionnaire, "Ah, I remember it well," which

Beth-El Historians

Marjorie Martin, class of 1927, with Julia Ray Work, class of 1913, and Jo Ruth, Beth-El Alumni Historian 1981 to 2016, Honorary Diploma Graduate of 1984, and Faculty 1974 to 1999.
Photo courtesy of Jo Ruth.

accompanied the 1982 alumni newsletter. The questionnaire asked graduates to share as many details of their student experiences at Deaconess Hospital or Beth-El Training/School of Nursing, as they could remember. The alumni came forward with their stories and drawings of the hospital campus.

They shared letters of admission, pictures, memorabilia, books, and even their uniforms. The collection expanded to the point that Beth-El Alumni and Beth-El School of Nursing held a celebration for their eightieth anniversary with a six-week display in the Smith Gallery of the Pioneers Museum, March 11 to April 29, 1984. Mayor Robert Isaac signed a Congratulatory Proclamation and the celebration opened with a gala reception at the Pioneers Museum. Now was the time for the school to celebrate, for who knew if there would be a centennial celebration? This collected history and memorabilia were the beginning of the Beth-El Alumni Archives and Beth-El School Archives.[117]

With unfailing determination, the director and faculty continued exploring ever-elusive opportunities for Beth-El students to obtain a Bachelor of Science in Nursing (BSN). Perhaps offering an associate's degree within the basic nursing program might be possible or perhaps, a post-diploma BSN opportunity would be acceptable. Possibilities included affiliation with a university or college in Colorado. Exploratory conversations with the University of Colorado at Colorado Springs (UCCS) were not fruitful. Loretto Heights College in Denver was another theoretical possibility for students to obtain a BSN following Beth-El graduation. The University of Southern Colorado hoped to continue their outreach program begun at Peterson Air Force Base. Mrs. Johns wrote in the 1981 Alumni Newsletter, "However, another group representing the administrators of all the local hospitals has now begun meeting and has recently sent letters to all state colleges and universities, inviting them to consider bringing a [BSN] program to our area.... If that does not bring forth some result, we at Beth-El are prepared to look into the feasibility of what it would take to become a degree-granting institution on our own." People of the city were again anxiously asking, "Will we have nurses in the future?"[118]

One year melded into the next as students and faculty worked together, mastering nursing knowledge, human caring, communication, technical skills, and critical thinking to meet future nursing and health care challenges. Never far from their thoughts and effort was the goal of offering a Bachelor of Science in Nursing degree for a hopeful and supportive community. The faculty and curriculum committees studied latest academic research, invited nursing leaders to conduct workshops, and worked with mentors from the National League for Nursing baccalaureate council. They discussed and reflected on nursing theorists and delved into conceptual frameworks. The foundation and structure of a new program began to take shape. The faculty stated, "The profession of nursing is founded upon four general concepts, that is: health, environment, the individual, and nursing. The faculty at Beth-El believes that a fifth concept basic to nursing is human caring...the central concept for the Beth-El program because the faculty believed human caring is the force that drives the other four concepts."[119] Jean Watson's developing nursing theory of human caring concepts was the basis for the faculty reflections and decisions.[120] With this foundation, talented faculty members completed development of the curriculum, core objectives, sub-concepts, course objectives, and related academic structure. The director, alumni, hospital administration, committed Colorado Springs benefactors, along with nurse supporters, worked tirelessly to build a moral and financial support base for a future baccalaureate program.

As all collaborative options failed to materialize, a dramatic development came in February 1985: The Beth-El Board of Trustees supported the Beth-El School's desire to move from diploma education to a baccalaureate degree, as a freestanding college of nursing. The Board of Memorial Hospital also concurred; however, the city referendums in 1949 and 1971 solidly maintained Colorado Springs citizen ownership of Beth-El School of Nursing. It was legally necessary to maintain a formal connection with the citizens. The two boards agreed; the Memorial Hospital treasurer would sit on a new Beth-El College Board, thus preserving a relationship with the city-owned hospital and citizens of Colorado Springs. The Hospital Board of Trustees also gave permission to change the name to **Beth-El College of Nursing** and to accept students into a BSN program in the fall of 1985.

As the faculty and students prepared for the baccalaureate degree, there were two more important aspects to consider. The diploma cap and graduate pin would be no longer appropriate for the BSN graduates. Tammy Palmer, class of 1984, eagerly redesigned the traditional cap, which had a front folded brim with five pleats in the back. She simplified the poufy top by removing the gathers and attaching a smoothly pleated cap body to the brim. The new cap lies flat and then folds into a neat box style. The traditional black, ¼-inch velvet band placed across the center of brim completed the cap. The faculty and students accepted the revised design as a "tip of the hat" to current fashion trends. The graduates of 1983 were the first to wear the newly designed cap. Students and graduates could choose to wear either cap. Tammy Palmer modeled the new cap while holding an infant during her pediatric nursing experience. The cover of the *Beth-El School of Nursing Catalogue, 1984-1985* featured this image. (See page 92.) However, it would only be a few years until nurses were not regularly wearing caps. No longer could they recognize an alumna of Beth-El from a distance.[121]

Simultaneously, faculty feverishly completed work required for accreditations from the North Central Association for Schools and Colleges, Colorado State Board of Nursing, and National League for Nursing granted accreditations as scheduled. Candidates for diploma and baccalaureate degrees would graduate from accredited programs. The current diploma students had an opportunity to choose graduation with a Diploma in 1987, or complete their education with a BSN. The *1985 Alumni Newsletter* included sample curriculum plans for the new baccalaureate students, former graduates, and other registered nurses (R.N.) who wished to complete a degree.[122]

[84] Lydia Dazy Hornbeck, Handmade Yearbook 1933, Unpublished: Colorado Springs, 1933.

[85] "Beth-El Purchase by City Approved," *Colorado Springs Gazette*, February 10, 1943.

[86] E. L. Mosley, City Manager, "Interim Report to Mayor and City Council," 1943.

[87] "Memorial Hospital Grown from Pioneer Institution," *Colorado Springs Gazette*, August 10, 1952.

[88] Dick Foster, "Council OKs Leasing of Ent as Olympic Training Site," *Colorado Springs Gazette*, March 22, 1977.

[89] "Plat Showing Property Owned by Bethel Hospital" Pikes Peak Library District, SCHMAP 362 110978 p 716, 1943.

[90] "Boiler Sized Overcoat," *Colorado Springs Gazette*, February 22, 1948.

[91] Mabel Meyer Bishop, "Beth-El Alumni Questionnaire" Binder 1946, Beth-El Alumni Collection, UCCS Archives.

[92] "Beth-El Nursing Faculty Sponsors Polio Workshop," *Colorado Springs Gazette*, July 24, 1949 Sec B 12.

[93] "Memorial Hospital Annex," *Colorado Springs Gazette*, February 22, 1948.

[94] "Observation Unit Conversion Alleviates Crowded Condition," *Colorado Springs Gazette*, February 22, 1948.

[95] Patricia Ann Jacobs, "Beth-El Alumni Questionnaire" Binder 1948, Beth-El Alumni Collection, UCCS Archives.

[96] Donahue, *Nursing the Finest Art*, 389.

[97] Doris Whitbeck, "Why No Funds? Beth-El Ask," *Colorado Springs Gazette*, April 1, 1949.

[98] "Spiffy Laboratory," *Colorado Springs Gazette*, December 5, 1950.

[99] Stewart's Photography, Memorial Hospital Entrance and West Wing. Pikes Peak Library District, Special Collection.

[100] Grace Bodenestine Heath, "Hear YE! Hear YE!"*Beth-El Alumni Newslettter* 1, no. 1 (October 1949).

[101] "Beth-El School of Nursing to Graduate class of 12," *Gazette Telegraph*, August 2, 1953.

[102] Douglas R. McKay, *UCCS—The First 25 Years: A Selective History* (Colorado Springs: University of Colorado, Colorado Springs, 1991), 23, 25.

[103] Carol Kenyon Grimm, "Beth-El Alumni Questionnaire" Binder 1956, Beth-El Alumni Collection, UCCS Archives.

[104] Wanda Bauder, "Beth-El Alumni Questionnaire" Binder 1958, Beth-El Alumni Collection, UCCS Archives.

[105] "Men in Nursing Historical Timeline," all nurses, http://allnurses.com/men-in-nursing/men-nursing-historical-96326.html (accessed June 29, 2014).

[106] "He Took Hold of Bootstrap and Lifted…," *Colorado Springs Gazette*, March 20, 1966.

[107] Beth-El Yearbook Committee, *Beth-El Yearbook* (Colorado Springs: Beth-El School of Nursing, 1968).

[108] Gene Birkhead, "McCleary, Dodge, Marshall Win: Voters Support Beth-El, 2 to 1," *Colorado Springs Sun*, April 7, 1971.

[109] Rick Hendren, "Urban, Memorial Projects Approved: Sondermann Gets Highest Vote Count,"

Colorado Springs Gazette, April 4, 1973.

[110] Anne C. Rinehart, Newsletter, Beth-El School of Nursing, Colorado Springs, April, 1974.

[111] "Ent Air Force Base Map" Peterson Air and Space Museum, Peterson Air Force Base, Colorado Springs, 2014.

[112] Beth-El Alumni Association, *Beth-El Alumni Newsletter,* Beth-El School of Nursing, Colorado Springs, 1975.

[113] L. Jean Johns, *Beth-El Alumni Newsletter,* Beth-El School of Nursing, Colorado Springs, 1976.

[114] Johns, *Beth-El Alumni Newsletter,* 1976.

[115] J. Robert Peters, *Beth-El Alumni Newsletter,* Beth-El School of Nursing, Colorado Springs, 1978.

[116] L. Jean Johns, *Beth-El Alumni Newsletter,* 1978.

[117] Beth-El Yearbook Committee, *Beth-El Chart Yearbook,* (Colorado Springs: Beth-El School of Nursing, 1983, 1984); Beth-El Alumni Association, *Alumni Newsletter,* Beth-El School of Nursing, Colorado Springs, 1982, 1983, 1984.

[118] L. Jean Johns, *Beth-El Alumni Newsletter,* 1981.

[119] Beth-El Faculty, "Overview of the Baccalaureate Program: Conceptual Framework," (Colorado Springs: Beth-El School of Nursing), 1989.

[120] Jean Watson, *Nursing: The Philosophy and Science of Caring* (Boulder: Colorado Associated University Press, 1985).

[121] *Beth-El School of Nursing Catalogue, 1984-1985* (Colorado Springs: Beth-El School of Nursing of Memorial Hospital), January 1984.

[122] Johns, *Beth-El Alumni Newsletter,* 1985.

Beth-El College of Nursing

10 North Farragut Avenue

1985–1992 Beth-El College of Nursing

The transition to a two-level building at 10 North Farragut provided a sense of reality to the accomplishment of moving forward to a bachelor's in nursing degree program. There was also enormous gratitude to all in the community who believed in and worked toward their collective vision to continue providing excellent nursing care and education that had begun with Deaconess Training School in 1904.

Beth-El School and College moved February 15, 1985, to a convenient and pleasant building. Memorial Hospital services and administration offices were rapidly expanding which required the hospital space Beth-El had occupied. Transitions are always complex and challenging; however, faculty and the community had actively worked for this opportunity for over 15 years and were ready and eager to move forward.[123]

Jean Johns, Director of Beth-El, invited current students and alumni to submit original drawings for a new pin. Proposals submitted by Radene Roberts, class of 1977, and Sue Hafey, class of 1987, were selected by the faculty and combined in the final design. The gold round pin retained the traditional red cross and added four interlocking rings placed around the center and arms of the cross. The rings signified the conceptual framework of Man, Health, Environment, and Nurse; a white enamel ring with the words Beth-El College of Nursing encircled the cross. A small gold laurel wreath ringed the perimeter.[124]

An Evolution of Beth-El Nursing Pins
1911–1922   1923–1944   1944–1987   1987–Present

The Beth-El School of Nursing held their Seventy-Ninth Annual and final diploma graduation for 11 students on May 22, 1987, at the Fine Arts

Center. Four of their classmates opted to complete nursing education with the new baccalaureate degree. Beth-El College of Nursing held the first Bachelor of Science in Nursing graduation on December 18, 1987. These four proud graduates joined 22 additional candidates for degrees at the first commencement on May 20, 1988, held at Benet Hill Center. Dr. Jean Watson, Dean of the University of the Colorado Health Sciences Center, delivered the address. The deep heritage of philanthropy, faith, progressive era of community, and nursing had collectively moved forward to provide the best care possible for citizens of Colorado Springs and the Pikes Peak region.[125]

As specialization in nursing practice and advances in medical treatments expanded, there were new demands for care from patients who now had opportunities for treatment as well as enhancement of health and wellness. Nurses needed advanced educational opportunities beyond diploma and BSN education. Beth-El responded to the community needs as they developed an RN to BSN program and added continuing education opportunities for innovative specialty areas. Once again, Beth El faculty and administration worked through creative, educational, and developmental hurdles to initiate a Master of Science in Nursing (MSN) program.

The Neonatal Nurse Practitioner (NNP) Program was the first example of specialization in the master's curriculum. The nurse practitioner movement began in the 1970s at the University of Colorado Health Sciences Center as a pediatric focus and extending into adult, neonatal, and family populations. In January 1986, Marcia London, NNP, a Beth-El faculty member, developed a nine and a half month program to prepare nurses for advanced practice positions in a new neonatal unit established by Memorial Hospital. This program continued until 2000 when it closed.[126] Graduates of this clinical specialty earned 18-semester undergraduate college credits and were eligible to take the Nurses Association of the American College of Obstetricians and Gynecologists Certification exam.[127]

[123] Johns, *Beth-El Alumni Newsletter*, 1985.
[124] "Artist Rendering of Beth-El BSN pin," Beth-El School of Nursing, Colorado Springs, 1986.
[125] "Beth-El School of Nursing Graduation Program," May 22, 1987; "Beth-El College of Nursing Graduation Program," May 18, 1987 (Colorado Springs: Beth-El School and College of Nursing), 1987.
[126] Mary Enzman Hines, letter, June 26, 2014.
[127] Johns, *Beth-El Alumni Newsletter*, 1985.

Beth-El College of Nursing and Health Science

2790 North Academy Boulevard
1992–1997

Beth-El College of Nursing was bursting at the seams with new educational offerings, students, and faculty. In January 1993, Beth-El moved to their North Academy location at the Offices at the Park just before the first students arrived for the new MSN degree program. Degree programs included clinical specialist and practitioner programs in adult health and neonatal nursing. A family nurse practitioner (FNP) and a post-master's practitioner program in adult health were also available. In 1995, a forensic nursing track, (the first in the country) and a holistic nursing program expanded curriculum offerings.[128]

In 1995, City Council received an unsolicited offer from Colorado Tech College (a for-profit institution) to purchase Beth-El. Dean Carol Schoffstall reported in the school newsletter, "In addition, UCCS has approached Beth-El about a possible merger between the two colleges. Those of us at Beth-El perceive that this would be a more congruent model to meet our ongoing educational and community service goals. City Council decided not to put the issue on the April ballot. We expect the issue to resurface for the November ballot." Students in all Beth-El programs excelled academically, clinically, and by taking leadership in the state and national student nurses organization. One nursing student was Commander of the UCCS ROTC unit. The Helene Fuld Fellowship selected a Beth-El student to represent Colorado for three consecutive years at their prestigious leadership program.[129]

Graduation on May 25, 1995, marked a milestone. Beth-El conferred degrees on 79 nursing graduates; 59 were basic BSN students, 20 were R.N.s who returned to Beth-El for their Bachelor of Science in Nursing degrees. The first eight graduates of the Master of Science in Nursing of Beth-El College of Nursing received their MSN degree. The graduates and community celebrated with a gala reception at the Antlers Doubletree Hotel.[130]

Beth-El students and the college met the requirements and achieved membership in the national nursing honor society November 8, 1995. Sigma Theta Tau International Honor Society of Nursing bestowed XI PHI Chapter charter on Beth-El College of Nursing and Health Sciences on April 28, 1996.[131]

Beth-El College of Nursing and Health Sciences secured North Central Accreditation summer of 1996 to offer a baccalaureate degree program in Health Care Services. The first health science major offered by the college was in emergency service.

Mary Enzman Hines reflected, "In 1997 the Clinical Nurse Specialist (CNS) holistic program began in addition to the adult focus, which was already implemented. The master's program again tapped the resources in the community and advanced the healthcare options for patients in the community."[132]

[128] Carole Schoffstall, Dean, Beth-El College of Nursing and Health Sciences at University of Colorado, Colorado Springs, *Alumni Newsletter*, 1994, 1995.

[129] Schoffstall, *Beth-El Alumni Newsletter*, 1995.

[130] Beth-El Alumni Association, *Beth-El Alumni Newsletter*, Spring issue No. 1, 1995.

[131] Beth-El Alumni Association, *Beth-El Alumni Newsletter*, Summer issue No. 2, 1996.

[132] Hines, letter, June 26, 2014.

Beth-El College of Nursing
and Health Sciences,
University of Colorado
Colorado Springs

1420 Austin Bluffs Parkway
1997–2014

Dean Carole Schoffstall proclaimed, "Our dream for the future of Beth-El became a reality on July 1, 1997. The college is now officially Beth-El College of Nursing and Health Sciences of University of Colorado at Colorado Springs."[133] June 24, 1997 city voters gave a resounding "YES" (70 percent to 30 percent) to the question of the merger with UCCS, as did City Council. The CU Board of Regents approved, and the Colorado Commission on Higher Education approved. The Colorado Legislature approved the operating budget, which Governor Roy Romer signed. The College was to remain at the Academy location until a building could be located on

135

campus. Not long after this, the college was again on the move, this time to the campus. Vail Hall, one of the new dormitories, did not yet have residents. In 1997–1999, UCCS transformed the first two floors into offices and added a newly established student health center for the campus. By 1999, the dorms filled with student residents, including Beth-El students. The university asked Beth-El to relocate to modular buildings located on the UCCS campus at 815 Eagle Rock Road, situated on the east side of North Nevada Avenue. As the UCCS campus expanded in 2003, Beth-El moved to a large building at 3955 Cragwood Drive (the university later changed the address to 3955 Regents Circle) at the corner of Austin Bluffs Parkway and Union Boulevard. The university remodeled the large building (previously built by Compassion International) and renamed it University Hall. In September 2003—after 20 years and 11 moves—the Beth-El College of Nursing and Health Sciences was now "at Home."

Beth-El College celebrated their Centennial with joy and a touch of disbelief. Had they made it 100 years? There was a wide range of events throughout 2004–2005 that featured aspects of their history and current achievements. Celebrations kicked off August 13, 2004, with a Centennial Gala dinner held at Beth-El College of Nursing and Health Sciences in University Hall. An Art and Healing Exhibit at Beth-El College of Nursing and Health Sciences was on display, followed by an Open House that took place August 16–20, 2004. Mayor Lionel Rivera signed a Centennial Proclamation on August 20, 2004. The Kraemer Family Library on the UCCS campus hosted a reception and an extensive historical display of

2004 Beth-El Centennial Celebrations
3955 Regents Circle, UCCS campus

Beth-El College of Nursing and Health Sciences in University Hall on the UCCS Campus

A large banner over the front entrance of the new home proudly proclaimed the Centennial Anniversary Celebration year.

Photo courtesy Joanne Ruth

images and nursing memorabilia. As Beth-El historian, I presented, "We Are Beth-El Nurses: 100 Years of Nursing at Beth-El School and College" on October 21, 2004. The final event of the celebration year was The Centennial Finale/Donor Thank You Event, Friday, August 5, 2005, held at Beth-El College of Nursing and Health Sciences.

In keeping with the trends on the healthcare scene, the faculty developed a post-Master Doctorate of Nursing Practice (DNP) that accepted students in the fall of 2007. The focus of this program was to educate doctoral-prepared nurse practitioners and clinical nurse specialists. This program was the first practice doctorate on the campus. The program offered students an opportunity to work with community experts along with faculty to develop their capstone projects. The first cohort of five DNP students graduated May 17, 2010. Clearly, the community connections were essential to the implementation of each of the options in the master's program, and eventually the DNP program.[134]

Nurse…Nurse…Do we have a Nurse?

Yes, we do have Beth-El nurses and health sciences professionals for our community. Thanks to dedicated nurses, the strong will of thousands of citizens, and farsighted benefactors, Beth-El College of Nursing and Health Sciences at University of Colorado Colorado Springs is thriving.

We are Beth-El Nurses:
A Heritage of Caring
at the Foot of Pikes Peak.

Students Modeling Beth-El Uniforms with Jo Ruth
As a member of the faculty, a 1984 Honorary Diploma recipient from Beth-El School of Nursing, Alumni Historian, and author of We are Beth-El Nurses: A Heritage of Nursing at the Foot of Pikes Peak, *I stand together with the students as we share a moment of joyful reflection following the Centennial Gala on August 13, 2004.*

Photo courtesy of John M. Rowland, class of 2006.

---

[133] Carole Schoffstall, *Beth-El Alumni Newsletter*, 1997.
[134] Hines, interview by Joanne Ruth, Colorado Springs, June 19, 2014.

Addendum
"Children's Pavilion"
The Visiting Nurse Association
Children's Ward and
Children's Pavilion at
Beth-El Hospital
1912–1914

Beth-El Hospital Children's Pavilion or "Annex"
1915–1927

"Nutrition Camp"
1928–1964

Marjorie Palmer Watt Nutrition School Annex Camp
1928–1964
Sponsored by Glockner/Penrose Hospital and
The Junior League of Colorado Springs

The Visiting Nurse Association Children's Ward and Children's Pavilion at Beth-El
1912–1914
Beth-El Hospital Children's Pavilion or "Annex"
1915–1927

Many single adults and families in Colorado Springs were living in poverty in the 1900s.

Often they were ill, without jobs, friends, or family to turn for help. As the number of the adults who suffered from tuberculosis expanded, caring progressive women and men of our nation and communities felt great concern for the health of the children. This universal concern for families and children was the impetus for Lillian Wald's pioneering Visiting Nurse movement at the Henry Street Settlement in New York City.[135]

An unnamed wealthy couple came from the East to Colorado Springs with hopes the gentleman would recover from his tuberculosis. However, this was not to be. Following his death, his wife, who understood the value of the visiting nurse movement, fervently believed that all families could benefit from a visiting nurse or a private nurse such as she afforded for her husband. She gave a generous donation to Reverend M. Taft, rector of St. Steven's Church, to establish a visiting nurse service for the poor of Colorado Spring.[136]

The District Nurse Association became a reality with this gift. In 1909, women of the church provided additional support to continue the visiting nurse service. The Board of Directors of the Associated Charities, Mrs. Wood's former Relief Society, offered office space and provided a uniform for the nurse. By

1911, the Colorado Springs District Nurse became one of the earliest formal Visiting Nurse Associations (VNA) in the United States. Their mission expanded as they provided services such as a "loan closet" for sickroom supplies and a diet kitchen to prepare broth for delivery to ill children and adults. They also prepared milk for sick infants.[137]

There was an additional concern for children who might be well but looked "sickly." What could the women do to prevent the children from "taking ill" with tuberculosis or other deadly childhood diseases?

Robert Koch had isolated the tubercle bacillus in 1882. During the turn of the century two European physicians, Niels Finsen, Auguste Rollier, and an American, John Harvey Kellogg, developed the use of heliotherapy therapies (prescribed exposure to sun light) as valuable treatments for bone and skin tuberculosis.[138] The tuberculin skin test, developed in 1907, aided in the identification of children who tested positive for tuberculosis although they did not appear to have symptoms of the disease.

Many folks believed children, identified as "pretubercular" might avoid developing tuberculosis if they received care similar to that found in popular sanatoriums. VNA nurses undoubtedly knew of the new health concept of "Preventoriums" recently established by Philanthropist Nathan Straus of Macy's Company in Lakewood, New Jersey in 1909.[139]

The Preventorium community, specially designed to house "sickly" children from crowded New York City tenements, might have seemed like a dream to the children. The combination of fresh air, the sunshine, good hygiene, healthful food, educational classes, and a rigid scheme of rest and planned exercise was sure to bring these children to robust health. The goal was for the children to develop a future "healthy lifestyle" as envisioned at the time. Some preventoriums provided additional medical and surgical treatment for children. Schools, churches, visiting nurses, and doctors made admission recommendations. As was the custom, there were also rigidly limited family visiting policies. This regimented, open-air lifestyle proved challenging to children and adults in preventoriums and sanatoriums alike; however, it was the best well-intentioned "cure" known in that day.[140]

Through a shared vision for the enhancement of current and future health of children in Colorado Springs, the Visiting Nurse Association Board developed a plan to benefit this broad health and community concern. The local Beth-El local Board of Managers and Florence E. Standish, Superintendent of the Deaconess Hospital, were eager to offer children's services at the new hospital on East Boulder Street. Their conversations evolved into a plan that included a Children's Ward and Children's Pavilion at Beth-El Hospital that were near completion.

Miss Olivia Caseceut, Chairman of the Children's Ward Committee, described their work in her 1914 annual report.

> In February 1912 the Visiting Nurse Association [VNA] opened a Children's Ward in a wing [east wing, first floor] of Beth-El Hospital, supplying a Head Nurse and paying to the Hospital $1.00 a day per patient

and a scale of charges for the use of the Operating room. A Pavilion in the grounds of the Hospital was soon built by the Association to care for all cases requiring out-of-door treatment. The hospital ward consisted of five-rooms with a total of twenty children's beds. The VNA built a small building at their expense. The Children's Pavilion was "required by the medical staff."[141]

The building was a simple wooden structure that faced southeast, built near the northeast hospital property line. It had an enclosed central dining room and nurse's office. Two open-air, covered sleeping porches, extended out at an angle on either end of the dining room to accommodate girls on one side and boys on the other. There was also an attached sun porch with a glider swing. A nurse, employed by the VNA and Beth-El nursing students, staffed the Children's Pavilion and Ward.

The 1913 VNA annual report for the Beth-El Children's Ward and Children's Pavilion included the following details of the care provided during the previous year.

As in all Children's Hospitals, the principle work at first has been in connection with throat cases. There have been 97 operations for removal of tonsils and adenoids but there have been operations for mastoids, eyes, appendicitis, tumors and others. Many

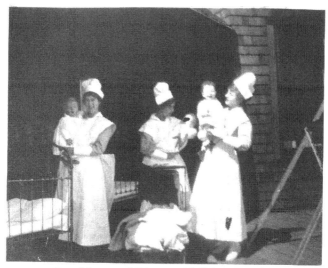

Sunshine and Happy Children on the Children's Pavilion Porch

Three Beth-El junior nursing students (no black band on the cap) enjoy holding and showing off their young patients on the Children's Pavilion sun porch.

Courtesy Margaretta M. Boas Collection, PPLD Library.

severe cases of typhoid, pneumonia, chorea, malnutrition, and diseases with formidable names that have been entirely unknown to the Committee and have led your Chairman to invest in a Medical Dictionary and Encyclopedia that she might learn something of them, and to know what measure of thankfulness we should feel because of our ability to help them. The Children's Ward league was started last year [1912] to encourage children of all ages to co-operate in the work of preventing and relieving sickness among the poor by examination and care in the Children's Ward.

Miss Leathem, a [1912] graduate of Beth-El who has been with children for a number of years, has been at the head of the Ward, performing faithfully and well all her dutys [sic], and untiring in her devotion to the children and in her efforts to make the training in Children's Nursing of valuable assistance to the undergraduate nurses of Beth-El, who have availed themselves of the opportunity thus offered by the work in the Ward.[142]

Six Children on Wooden Glider Swing

The high-backed, double glider was a popular diversion for patients and nurses alike. When the children were well enough to be out of the Children's Ward, they slept, ate, and played in the open-air sunshine of the Children's Pavilion. Courtesy Pikes Peak Library District.

The children and students alike gathered on the grounds to sit on the two-seat porch glider. They documented their fun with small Brownie box cameras.[143] At the close of 1914, the VNA was unable to raise sufficient funds to cover care for children who had no other financial support. To "secure its permanence and increased usefulness to the community," the VNA leadership saw no other option than to transfer the Children's Ward and Pavilion to Beth-El Hospital. The hospital continued to operate the Children's Ward. There are no primary records available, which describe how long the hospital maintained active care of children in the Pavilion. However, Esther Tandy Paden, a student who graduated in 1920 remembered, "a temporary building that housed tubercular children was there" at that time.[144] Another student, Freda Morris Disch, also a 1920 graduate, remembered, "The Children's Ward was in the basement—right wing [east wing] front [half of the ward]. In the spring, all patients able to be moved were taken to the Pavilion for the summer."[145] Margaret Boucher Waddel, class of 1927, related she worked days about six weeks in 1926, caring for about 14 young women housed in the building. Margaret added that she gained 15 pounds, "which was lost as soon as I was back on regular duty—we served nourishing, rich food to the girls."[146]

As the years passed, most of the staff and students lost knowledge of the name "Children's Pavilion." They simply referred to the aging, odd little building as the "Annex," which was used as storage or accommodations for rare summer, open-air sleeping experiences.

Marjorie Palmer Watt Nutrition School Annex Camp 1928–1964
Sponsored by Glockner/Penrose Hospital and the Junior League of Colorado Springs

As the preventorium movement gained nationwide popularity in 1923, General Palmer's daughters Miss Dorothy Palmer and Mrs. Marjorie Palmer (Henry C). Watt opened a nutrition service in Marjorie's home. They served children who appeared undernourished, underweight, and who were from families who had limited resources. Soon they needed the additional space; Sister Mary of Glockner Hospital furnished an attractive building on Glockner Hospital grounds to care for the children.[147]

The Glockner building, later known as Seton Hall, served the Seton School of Nursing, Penrose Hospital, Colorado Springs.

Mrs. Watt and Miss Palmer, who continued to partially endow the endeavor, were joined by the Junior League[148] and a board of physicians and laymen who carried the mission forward. In 1928, the Children's Pavilion building, which began as a VNA Preventorium in 1912, was available and seemed a natural asset to this new community endeavor. The National Board of Hospitals, Homes, and Deaconess Work of the Methodist Episcopal Church, transferred ownership of the building to the Nutrition Camp authorities. The Marjorie Palmer Watt Nutrition School Annex Camp renewed care of the children of Colorado Springs.[149] Beth-El Hospital and nursing students had no further formal association with the facility after 1928.

The newly formed Junior League of Colorado Springs, along with the Glockner-Penrose Hospital took the lead in sponsoring the Nutrition Camp. Citizens of Colorado Springs continued their active support of the Nutrition Camp School through hugely popular Nu-Ca-Zar benefits as well as other community fundraising efforts. Admission to the facility was through the recommendation of a public health nurse, school nurse, or doctor. Health promotion and illness prevention consisted of good food, prescribed exercise, open-air living in the sunshine, and a regimented lifestyle. There were also public health nurses, medical doctors, and clinical nurses who offered free examinations, medical care, and health instruction. Academic teachers held open-air classes with regular school desks placed on the sun porch. The Nutrition Camp invited families to visit on a strict schedule as determined by the staff. The local newspapers published intermittent articles and pictures of the children involved in activities at the Nutrition Camp.

In 1958, the Nutrition Camp Board of Directors refocused their efforts to offer a Nutrition Camp Pediatric Clinic held in conjunction with the City and County Health Department. As new treatment modalities became available for childhood illness, and healthcare practices and social norms evolved, the Pediatric Clinic moved out of the Health Department setting to Penrose Hospital in June of 1964.[150]

[135] Lillian D. Wald, *The House on Henry Street* (New York: Henry Holt and Company, 1915).

[136] Carrie Lee Schwartz, "Report of the President," Annual Meeting Visiting Nurse Association Colorado Springs, November 15, 1956. Report held by Special Collections, Pikes Peak Library District, Colorado Springs.

[137] Ibid.

[138] Barbara Brodie, "Children of the Sun," *Windows in Time,* (Charlottesville, VA: The Eleanor Crowder Bjoring Center for Nursing Historical Inquiry. Vol. 23 Issue 2, October 2015), 9.

[139] Cynthia A. Connolly, "Nurses: The Early Twentieth Century Tuberculosis Preventorium's Connecting Link," *Nursing History Review,* (New York: Springer Publishing Company, Vol. 10, 2002), 127–157.

[140] Ibid.

[141] Schwartz, "Report of the President," 1956, 3.

[142] Olivia Caseceut, "1914 Annual Report of the Children's Ward Committee," Report of the President Annual Meeting, Colorado Springs: Visiting Nurse Association. November 15, 1956), 3.

[143] Marjorie Henderson Martin, "Alumni Scrapbooks 1973, Vol. I, 52" Colorado Springs: Beth-El Alumni Association.

[144] Esther Tandy Paden, "Beth-El Alumni Questionnaire," 1982 letter, Beth-El Alumni Collection Notebook 1920, Beth-El Alumni Collection, University of Colorado, Colorado Springs (UCCS) Archives.

[145] Freda Morris Disch, "Beth-El Alumni Questionnaire," Notebook 1920, Beth-El Alumni Collection, UCCS Archives.
[146] Margaret Boucher Waddel, "Beth-El Alumni Questionnaire," Notebook 1927, Beth-El Alumni Collection, UCCS Archives.
[147] "Penrose-St. Francis Health Services," http://www/penrosestfrancis.org/index.php?s=113 (accessed August 5, 2008).
[148] "Junior League of Colorado Springs," http://www/healthycoloradan.com/junior-league-of-colorado-springs/ (accessed September 12, 2015).
[149] Glockner Training School Yearbook Committee. "Nutrition Camp School," *1923 Glockner Training School Yearbook*, (Colorado Springs, 1923) held by Special Collections, Pikes Peak Library District.
[150] "Pediatric Clinic Moved," *Gazette Telegraph*, June 4, 1964.

Combined Timeline of the History of Beth-El College of Nursing and Health Sciences University of Colorado Colorado Springs and UCHealth Memorial Hospital

The History of Ecumenical and Protestant Hospitals in Colorado Springs prior to the Deaconess/Beth-El/ Memorial Hospital Era

1888–1890 Eleanor House, which was located on the northwest corner of Columbia and Weber, was established by Mrs. Clinton (Eleanor) Collier and a group of concerned women.

1890–1894 Bellevue, a new three story wooden building built for Eleanor House patients was located on South Institute Street on the crest of the hill east of St. Francis Hospital, which was on Pikes Peak Avenue.

1894–1900 Unknown use of building.

1900–1902 National Deaconess Sanatorium, a.k.a. The New Bellevue Sanatorium was owned and operated by the National Deaconess Sanatorium and Hospital Society of Chicago.

1902–1903 A local group called Bellevue Hospital Association considered buying the hospital but in the end declined to do so.

(This concluded the pre Beth-El/Memorial era)

1903–1904 Mrs. William (Belle) Lennox and Mrs. A.C. (Frances) Peck, who lived in Denver at the time, organized a group of women of the community who were concerned about the need for a Protestant hospital. The Woman's Home Missionary Society (WHMS) of the Colorado Conference of the Methodist Episcopal Church was interested and set about to buy the Bellevue building.

1904–1911 Colorado Conference Deaconess Hospital and Training School was established by the Woman's Home Missionary Society of the Colorado Conference of the Methodist Episcopal Church. Mrs. Lennox was elected President of the local Board of Managers. Mrs. A.C. Peck attended every board meeting and named the new hospital Bethel, a Hebrew word meaning "House of God." Mrs. Peck was the guiding light of the group. She wrote the words and music of the dedicatory hymn.

1911–1922 Beth-El Hospital and Training School
The Woman's Home Missionary Society of the

Colorado Conference of the Methodist Episcopal Church and the local Board of committed women continued their work.

1912—Children's Pavilion built in collaboration with the Visiting Nurses Association.

1916—Nurses Home served as the formal location of the school and nurses' residence.

1918—Observation or Contagion Hospital (City/County owned) was staffed by Beth-El Students.

1922–1943 Beth-El General Hospital and School of Nursing Ownership of the hospital was transferred to the Board of Hospitals, Homes and Deaconess Work of the Methodist Episcopal Church.

1926—National Methodist Episcopal Sanatorium for Tuberculosis was opened in a new three-story building east of the Nurses Home on Boulder Street.

1928—Idlewold Nurses Home, a former TB sanatorium, was the home for Senior Nursing students. Located at 311 North Logan Avenue, it became the Ronald McDonald House on February 14, 1987.

1937—Daniels Hall, Crippled Children's Recreation Hall and activity center for nursing students. The school library was located in the east side of the building.

1943–1985 Memorial Hospital and Beth-El School of Nursing

1949—Colorado Springs citizens vote to support Beth-El School of Nursing.

1952—West wing opened and ground floor,

front main entrance remodeled.

1953—First two African-American women graduated from Beth-El School of Nursing.

1966—First two men graduated from Beth-El School of Nursing.

1971—Colorado Springs Citizens again vote two to one to continue their support of Beth-El.

1974—The Nurses Home and Daniels Hall demolished and later the next year the Observation Hospital was demolished to make way for new hospital construction.

1974–1977—First seven-story patient tower was erected on the site of the Contagion Hospital. The original Beth-El building was enclosed inside a new façade and the interior remodeled. A three-story parking garage was located on the Nurses Home site.

1973–1977—Beth-El School of Nursing moved four times to accommodate hospital construction.

1985–1992 The School became Beth-El College of Nursing Located at 10 North Farragut. Memorial Hospital continued to expand to accommodate the health care needs of the citizens of Colorado Springs.

1987—Last class of Diploma students and first BSN students graduated from Beth-El.

1992–1997 The college became Beth-El College of Nursing and Health Sciences in 1995. The College was located at 2790 North Academy Boulevard. Initially, Beth-El offered Master of Science in Nursing with a focus in Adult Nurse Practitioner/Clinical Specialist or Neonatal Nurse Practitioner/Clinical Specialist tracts. The College also established a

Forensic Nursing Master of Science and a Holistic Nursing Clinical Specialist program.

1996 First class of Master of Science in Nursing students graduated from Beth-El College of Nursing and Health Sciences. The graduation service was held at the First United Methodist Church, which has been the traditional site of graduation for many years.

1997 In a city vote the citizens gave Beth-El College permission to merge with the University of Colorado, Colorado Springs; now known as **Beth-El College of Nursing and Health Sciences University of Colorado Colorado Springs.**

1997 Memorial Hospital opened the second seven-story patient tower on the former site of the El Paso County Department of Health, which was adjacent to the first patient tower.

1997–1999 Beth-El College relocated to Vail Hall on UCCS campus.

1999 Beth-El College relocated to the modular buildings at 815 Eagle Rock Road on the UCCS campus.

2003 Beth-El College relocated to University Hall, which is on the corner of Austin Bluff Boulevard and Union Boulevard (3955 Regents Circle). This building, which is, for now, our *permanent home*, provides expanded classroom and faculty space.

2007 Doctorate of Nursing Practice (DNP) was established and other programs expanded.

2004–2010 A seven–story parking garage was constructed on the northeast section of the hospital at 1400 East Boulder. The previous parking garage located on Boulder Street (where the Nurses Home was originally located) was torn down to make way for the **Children's Hospital** addition to the hospital. **Memorial Hospital North** opened at 4050 Briargate Parkway. The main campus is now known as **UCHealth Memorial Hospital Central.**

2010 Doctorate of Nursing Practice first cohort of seven students graduated from Beth-El College of Nursing and Health Science at UCCS.

2012 Memorial Hospital leased by a citizen vote to University of Colorado Health (UCHealth) for 40 years. Colorado Springs Health Foundation formed to grant money received from the revenue to public health initiatives across El Paso and Teller Counties.

2015 Helen and Arthur E. Johnson Beth-El College of Nursing and Health Sciences University of Colorado Colorado Springs. The CU Board of Regents recognized the Denver-based Johnson Foundation's $8 million endowed gift by renaming the College of Nursing and Health Sciences at UCCS.

Joanne Ruth, M.S., Beth-El Alumni Historian and Retired Beth-El Faculty1973-1999

BIBLIOGRAPHY

Bauder, Wanda. "Beth-El Alumni Questionnaire." Colorado Springs, 1958.

Beth-El Alumni Association. *Alumni Newsletter.* Colorado Springs, 1975.

—. *Alumni Newsletter* . Colorado Springs, 1982, 1983, 1984.

—. *Alumni Newsletter.* Colorado Springs, 1981.

—. *Alumni Newsletter.* Colorado Springs, 1995.

—. *Alumni Newsletter.* Colorado Springs, 1996.

Beth-El Hospital. *Procedure Manual Beth-El Hospital.* Colorado Springs: Donated by Mary Reed Green, class of 1935.

—. "The Beth-El Hospital Bulletin." December 1929.

Beth-El School of Nursing. "Beth-El Faculty Overview: The Philosophy and Science of Caring." Colorado Springs, 1989.

Beth-El School of Nursing. "History of Beth-El School of Nursing." Paper held by Colorado State Board of Nursing, unknown author,

Colorado Springs, c1928.

Beth-El Training School. "1912 Graduation Program." Colorado Springs, 1912.

Beth-El Yearbook Committee. *Beth-El Chart Yearbook*. Colorado Springs, 1983, 1984.

Beth-El Yearbook Committee. *Beth-El Yearbook*. Colorado Springs, 1968.

Beth-El Yearbook Committee. *TPR* Beth-El Yearbook. Colorado Springs, 1928.

—. *TPR* Beth-El Yearbook. Colorado Springs: Beth-El School of Nursing, 1930.

—. *TPR* Beth-El Yearbook, 1926.

Birkhead, Gene. *Colorado Springs SUN*. Colorado Springs, April 7, 1971.

Bishop, Mabel Meyer. "Beth-El Alumni Questionnaire." Colorado Springs, 1946.

Brodie, Barbara. "Children of the Sun: Heliotherapy and Tubercular Children." *Windows in Time*, Volume 23, Issue 2, October, 2015.

Burkhart, Dorothy Hamilton. "Beth-El Alumni Questionnaire." Colorado Springs, 1938.

Campbell, Arleene Prentice. "Beth-El Alumni Questionnaire." Colorado Springs, 1942.

Colorado State Board of Nurse Examiners. "Report of Beth-El School of Nursing visit." Denver, 1931.

—. *Reports*. 1929–1931 and 1939.

Deaconess Bureau of the Woman's Home Missionary Society of the Colorado Conference of the Methodist Episcopal Church. "Minutes," Denver, 1908.

—. Minutes. 1909.

—. Minutes. Denver, 1911

Deaconess Hospital Training School. "Deaconess Hospital Training School Report to Colorado State Board of Nurse Examiners." Colorado Springs, 1905.

Deaconess Hosptial Training School. "Deaconess Hospital Training School Report to the Colorado State Board of Nurse Examiners." Offical Report, Denver, 1906.

Disch, Freda Morris. "Beth-El Alumni Questionnaire," Addendum. Colorado Springs, 1920.

Donahue, M. Patricia. *Nursing the Finest Art: An Illustrated History.* Saint Louis: The C.V. Mosby Company, 1985.

Egan, Timothy. *The Worst Hard Time: the untold story of those who survived the great American dust bowl.* New York: Houghton Mifflin Co, 2006.

Foster, Dick. *Gazette.* "Council OKs Leasing of Ent as Olympic Training Site." Colorado Springs, March 22, 1977.

Gazette. "He Took Hold of Bootstrap and Lifted" Colorado Springs, March 20, 1966.

—. "Memorial Hospital Grown from Pioneer Institution." Colorado Springs, August 10, 1952.

—. "Observation Unit Conversion Alleviates Crowded Condition." Colorado Springs, February 22, 1948.

—. "Spiffy Laporatory." Colorado Springs, December 5, 1950.

—. "Boiler Sized Overcoat." Colorado Springs, February 22, 1948.

Goldmark, Josephine. *Nursing and Nursing Education in the United States*. New York: The MacMillan Company, reprinted by Garland Publishing, 1923, reprinted 1984.

Grimm, Carol Gibson. "Beth-El Alumni Questionnaire." Colorado Springs, 1956.

Hall, Irene Neese. "Beth-El Alumni Questionnaire," Addendum. Colorado Springs, 1932.

Health, Grace Bodenestine. "Hear YE! Hear YE!" *Beth-El Newsletter*, October 1949: Volume I Number 1.

Hill, Esther Green. *Beth-El Chart Yearbook*. Colorado Springs, 1992.

Hines, Mary Enzman, interview by Joanne Ruth. Professor Emeritus, University of Colorado Colorado Springs, Beth-El College of Nursing and Health Sciences (June 19, 2014).

Jacobs, Patricia Ann. "Beth-El Alumni Questionnaire." Colorado Springs, 1948.

Johns, L. Jean. *Beth-El Alumni Newsletter*. Colorado Springs, 1976.

—. *Beth-El Alumni Newsletter*. Colorado Springs, 1978.

—. *Beth-El Alumni Newsletter*. Colorado Springs, 1985.

Kalisch, Phyilip A. and Beatrice J. Kalisch. *The Changing Image of the Nurse*. Menlo Park: Addison-Wesley, 1987.

Lancaster, Barbara Rose Standish, 1942 Alumna, interview by Jo Ruth, Beth-El School of Nursing (1983-2014).

Local Board of Managers of the Deaconess Hospital. "Local Board Minutes, Book 2." Colorado Springs: Woman's Home Missionary Society of the Colorado Springs Methodist Episcopal Church. May 3, 1909.

Martin, Marjorie Henderson. *Alumni Scrapbooks, I, II, III, IV*. Colorado Springs, Colorado: Beth-El Alumni Association, 1973.

McKay, Douglas R. *UCCS-The First 25 Years: A Selective History*. Colorado Springs: University of Colorado at Colorado Springs, 1991.

Mosley, L.E.L. "Letter from Colorado Springs City Manager." January 19, 1943.

—. "Plat Showing Property Owned by Bethel Hospital." Pikes Peak Library District, Colorado Springs, 1943.

Nanninga, Sherry L. *Built with Women's Hands: A Deaconess Hospital in Colorado Springs 1904-1912*. Master Thesis, Denver: Iliff School of Theology, 1994

National League of Nursing Education. "Standard Curriculum for School of Nursing." *Committee on Education, Council of the National League of Nursing Education*. Baltimore, 1919.

Nutting, M. Adelaid, Introduction to S*tandard Curriculum for School of Nursing by the Committee on Education of the National League of Nursing Education*. Baltimore, Waverly Press, 1919.

Ormes, Mauly D. and Eleanor R. *The Book of Colorado Springs*. Colorado Springs: The Dentan Printing Co., 1933.

Paden, Esther Tandy. "Beth-El Alumni Questionnaire." Colorado Springs, 1920.

Peck, Florence. "History of Beth-El Hospital." *TPR* Beth-El Yearbook, Colorado Springs, 1923.

—. "Beth-El Hymn." Denver 1912.

Penney, Ruth E. A. Class of 1919, "Memory of Armistice Day, November, 11, 1918." Find in 1919 section of Beth-El Collection, Binder, University of Colorado, Colorado Springs Archives, Beth-El Alumni Collection, 1983.

Peters, J. Robert. *Beth-El Alumni Newsletter.* Colorado Springs, 1978.

Peterson Air and Space Museum. "Ent Air Force Base Map." Colorado Springs, 2014.

Rudolph, Katie. "The Influenza Pandemic of 1918: A Colorado Springs Timeline." *Doctors, Disease, and Dying in the Pikes Peak Region.* Colorado Springs: Pikes Peak Library District, 2012.

Ruth, Joanne F. "Note." 2014.

—. *Beth-El Alumni Newsletter.* 1992

Rutherford, Opel Stanford, Class of 1922, interview by Jean Johns, (c1986).

Schneider, Dorothy Schneider and Carl J Schneider. *American Women in the Progressive Era, 1900-1920.* New York: Anchor Books, Doubleday, 1993.

Schoffstall, Carole. *Beth-El Alumni Newsletter.* 1994.

—. *Beth-El Alumni Newsletter.* 1995.

—. *Beth-El Alumni Newsletter.* 1997.

Smith, Ollie J. "Beth-El Woman's Board Yesterday and Today." Speech written by Ollie J. Smith, Secretary of Beth-El Woman's Colorado Springs Board of the Colorado Conference of the

Woman's Home Missionary Society of the Methodist Episcopal Church of Colorado Springs, 1943.

Standish, Barbara Lancaster and Robert, interview by Jo Ruth. "Photo Albumn Conversation," (July 9, 1983).

Standish, Florence E. "Letter in 'Round Robin' Alunmi Newsletter." Mable E. Smith, Class of 1912, editor, 1937.

Thornton, Marie Robb. "Beth-El Alumni Questionnaire." Colorado Springs, 1935.

Vosler, Dorothy Schwab. "Beth-El Alumni Questionnaire." Colorado Springs 1946.

Watson, Jean. *Nursing:The Philosophy and Science of Caring*. Boulder: Colorado Associated University Press, 1985.

Welsome, Eileen. *Deep Roots, Aspen Pointe and Colorado Springs, Together Since 1875*. Colorado Springs: Aspen Point, 2013.

Whitbeck, Doris. "Why No Funds? Beth-El Ask." *Gazette*. Colorado Springs, April 1, 1949.

Wood, Almira. "A Review of Thirteen Years' Work." *Colorado Springs Weekly Gazette*, February 4, 1988.

Woolley, Mildred Kane. Letter, May 2014, Beth-El Alumni Collection Binder, 1942.

Work, Julia Ray and Margaret Glew. *History of Memorial Hospital and Beth-El School of Nursing 1904-1963*. Colorado Springs: Beth-El Alumnae Association, 1963.

Bibliography for Children's Pavilion and Nutrition Camp Addendum

Brodie, Barbara. "Children of the Sun," *Windows in Time.* Charlotte: Eleanor Crowder Bjoring Center for Nursing Historical Inquiry. October, 2015

Caseceut, Olivia. "1914 Annual Report of the Children's Ward Committee," *Report of the President Annual Meeting,* Colorado Springs: Visiting Nurses Association. November 15, 1956.

Connolly, Cynthia A. "Nurses: The Early Twentieth Century Tuberculosis Preventorium's Connecting Link," *Nursing History Review.* New York: Springer Publishing Company. Vol. 10, 2002.

Disch, Freda Morris. "Beth-El Alumni Questionnaire." Colorado Springs, 1920.

Gazette Telegraph. "Pediatric Clinic Moved." Colorado Springs, June 4, 1964.

Glockner Training School Yearbook Committee. "Nutrition Camp School," *1923 Glockner Training School Yearbook,* Colorado Springs, 1923.

Martin, Marjorie Henderson. *Alumni Scrapbooks, Vol. I. II.* Colorado Springs: Beth-El Alumni Association, 1973.

Paden, Esther Tandy. "Beth-El Alumni Questionnaire." 1982 letter. Colorado Springs, 1920.

Waddel, Margaret Boucher. "Beth-El Alumni Questionnaire." Colorado Springs, 1920.

Wald, Lillian D. *The House on Henry Street.* New York: Henry Holt and Company, 1915.

PHOTO GALLERY REFERENCE

Dedication Image Reference

Page ii—1920 Beth-El junior student preparing to weigh a newborn baby in the nursery workroom. Beth-El Hospital, Hand-tinted glass positive slide. Beth-El Alumni Collection, UCCS Archives.

Narrative Images References

Page 9—Mrs. Peck, Beth-El Alumnac Scrapbooks Vol. I 3. Beth-El Alumni Collection, UCCS Archives.

Page 9—Mrs. Lennox, htpp://lennoxhouse.com/history/aspx?type=w Accessed 01-Oct-2015.

Page 14—The Colorado Conference Deaconess. Beth-El Alumnae Scrapbooks Vol. I 1. Beth-El Alumni Collection, UCCS Archives.

Page 15— "Old Deaconess" Nursing Staff. Beth-El Alumnae Scrapbooks Vol. III 1. Beth-El Alumni Collection, UCCS Archives.

Page 20—Julia Work and high-spirited friends in 1910, Julia Ray Work collection, Beth-El Alumni Collection, UCCS Archives.

Page 23—Florence E. Standish. Florence E Standish collection, courtesy of Barbara Standish Lancaster, Beth-El Alumnae Scrapbooks Vol. II 65. Beth-El Alumni Collection, UCCS Archives.

Page 28—Julia Work Holding Baby 1915. Julia Ray Work collection, Beth-El Alumni Collection, UCCS Archives.

Page 29—Beth-El Hospital 1922. Beth-El Alumni Collection, UCCS Archives.

Page 31—1920 Student Nurses Gather on a Sun Porch. Beth-El Alumnae Scrapbooks Vol. I 54. Beth-El Alumni Collection, UCCS Archives.

Page 33—1912 Children's Pavilion. Julia Ray Work collection, Beth-El Alumni Collection, UCCS Archives.

Page 35—1924 Beth-El Alumnae Association, Beth-El Alumnae Scrapbooks Vol. I 55. Beth-El Alumni Collection, UCCS Archives.

Page 39—1920 Nurses Home, Beth-El Hospital, Beth-El Hospital, hand-tinted positive glass slide, Beth-El Alumni Collection, UCCS Archives.

Page 40—1920 Students in classroom with their instructors, Beth-El Hospital, hand-tinted positive glass slide. Beth-El Alumni Collection, UCCS Archives.

Page 45—Student nurses pose with "Naky" in the Operating Room, Pikes Peak Library District, Special Collection.

Page 47—1920 Nursery with Nurses and Dr. Timmons, Beth-El Hospital hand-tinted positive glass slide. Beth-El Alumni Collection, UCCS Archives.

Page 51—1929 Beth-El General Hospital. *TPR* Yearbook 1929, 6. Beth-El Alumni Collection, UCCS Archives.

Page 53—1926 National Methodist Episcopal Sanatorium for Tuberculosis. Beth-El Alumnae Scrapbooks Vol. I 28. Beth-El Alumni Collection, UCCS Archives.

Page 55—1931 Glee Club *TPR* 1931, 50. Also in Sally Brawner's collection, class of 1933. Beth-El Alumni Collection, UCCS Archives.

Page 56—Beth-El Hymn. France E. Peck, Beth-El Alumni Collection, UCCS Archives.

Page 57—1931 Idlewold Senior Dorm. TPR Yearbook 1931, 31. Beth-El Alumni Collection, UCCS Archives.

Page 65—1920 Beth-El Hospital Parlor. Beth-El Alumnae Scrapbooks Vol. I 5. Beth-El Alumni Collection.

Page 68—1942 Nursing Rounds, "Bulletin: Beth-El School of Nursing Affiliated with Memorial Hospital 1944–1947," 3. Grace Bodenstine Heath collection, Beth-El Alumni Collection, UCCS Archives.

The Photo Gallery References

Page 73—Beth-El Alumnae Association 1926 Formal Portrait. Beth-El TPR Yearbook 1926,74.

Page 73—Julia Ray Work. 1926, Beth-El Alumnae Scrapbooks Vol. I 68. Beth-El Alumni Collection, UCCS Archives.

Page 74—1904 Deaconess Hospital. Beth-El Alumnae Scrapbooks Vol. I 1. Beth-El Alumni Collection, UCCS Archives.

Page 74—c1912 A Lighthearted Moment for the Camera. Julia Ray Work collection, Beth-El Alumni Collection, UCCS Archives.

Page 75—1909 Beth-El Hospital Unfinished. Florence E. Standish collection, Beth-El Alumni Collection, UCCS Archives.

Page 75—1923 View of Beth-El Hospital. Beth-El Alumnae Scrapbooks Vol. I 55. Beth-El Alumni Collection, UCCS Archives.

Page 76—"Airplane view of Beth-El General Hospital and Sanatorium." (Newspaper headline and image, probably from a *Gazette Telegraph* special edition c1927–1930.) Beth-El Alumnae Scrapbooks Vol. I. 5. Beth-El Alumni Collection, UCCS Archives.

Page 77—Beth-El Hospital. Circa 1923. Beth-El Alumni Collection, UCCS Archives.

Page 77—1984 Looking South from the South Patient Tower. Courtesy Jo Ruth, Beth-El Alumni Collection, UCCS Archives.

Page 78—1915 Florence E. Standish's Nob Hill Lodge Sanatorium. Florence E. Standish collection, Beth-El Alumni Collection, UCCS Archives.

Page 78—Nob Hill Lodge. Beth-El *TPR* Yearbook 1931, 16. Beth-El Alumni Collection, UCCS Archives.

Page 79—1920 Student Nurses Room. Beth-El Hospital, hand-tinted positive glass slide. Beth-El Alumni Collection, UCCS Archives.

Page 79—1920 Living Room of Nurses Home. Beth-El Hospital hand-tinted positive glass slide. Beth-El Alumni Collection, UCCS Archives.

Page 80—1926 Christmas for the Students. Beth-El

Alumnae Scrapbooks 1973, Vol. I 6. Beth-El Alumni Collection, UCCS Archives.

Page 80—1925 Beth-El Basketball Team. Beth-El *TPR* Yearbook 1925, 5. Beth-El Alumni Collection, UCCS Archives.

Page 81—1920s Children's Ward on first floor East Wing. Beth-El Hospital, hand-tinted positive glass slide. Beth-El Alumni Collection, UCCS Archives.

Page 81—1931 Sanatorium Open Air and Sun Therapy. Evangeline Dean Deyo photo collection with Alumni Questionnaire. Also in Beth-El Alumnae Scrapbooks Vol. I 28. Beth-El Alumni Collection, UCCS Archives.

Page 82—1920 Preparing the Operating Room. Beth-El Hospital, hand-tinted positive glass slide. Beth-El Alumni Collection, UCCS Archives.

Page 82—1927 A Patient and OR Team. Beth-El *TPR* Yearbook 1927, 74. Beth-El Alumni Collection, UCCS Archives.

Page 83—1920 Special Diet Kitchen. Beth-El Hospital, hand-tinted positive glass slide. Beth-El Alumni Collection, UCCS Archives.

Page 83—1928 Patients and a Student Nurse on the "San" Roof. Beth-El Alumnae Scrapbooks Vol. I 28. Beth-El Alumni Collection, UCCS Archives.

Page 84—1913 Children at the Children's Pavilion. Julia Ray Work collection. Beth-El Alumni Collection, UCCS Archives.

Page 84—1928 Nutrition Camp Children Exercising for Health. *Gazette Telegraph*, May 20, 1928, Pikes Peak Library District, Special Collections.

Page 85—1936 Two Beth-El Babies Born 24 Hours Apart. *The Beth-El Hospital Bulletin*, 1936, 5. Martha Cogswell Thoman collection. Also in Beth-El Alumnae Scrapbooks Vol. II 29. Beth-El Alumni Collection, UCCS Archives.

Page 85—1916 "Mary Stewart's Last Baby Case," Mary Stewart collection. Beth-El Alumni Collection, UCCS Archives.

Page 86—1931 "Our Hospital" poem written by Sylvia (Sally) Lamprecht Boggs. Beth-El *TPR* Yearbook 1931,7. Beth-El Alumni Collection, UCCS Archives.

Page 87—c1953 New Front Entrance to the Hospital. Beth-El Alumnae Scrapbooks Vol. I 4. Beth-El Alumni Collection, UCCS Archives.

Page 87—The Special Care Nursery. Circa 1966. Beth-El Alumnae Scrapbooks Vol. I 10. Beth-El Alumni Collection, UCCS Archives.

Page 87—Beth-El Student with Her Instructor. Circa 1966. Beth-El Alumnae Scrapbooks Vol. I 38. Beth-El Alumni Collection, UCCS Archives.

Page 88—1962 Student Room. Beth-El Alumnae Scrapbooks Vol. I 7. Beth-El Alumni Collection, UCCS Archives.

Page 89—1996 Master of Science in Nursing Graduates. *The Beth-El Chart 1997*, 36. Beth-El Alumni Collection, UCCS Archives.

Page 89—1996 Alumni Homecoming. *The Beth-El Chart 1997*, 44. Beth-El Alumni Collection, UCCS Archives.

Page 90—1926 Emma Brace Admiring a Baby. Beth-El Alumnae Scrapbooks Vol. I 59. Beth-El Alumni Collection, UCCS Archives.

Page 91—1981 Donna Modisett Admiring a Baby. Beth-El School of Nursing catalog cover, 1981–1983, Beth-El Alumni Collection, UCCS Archives.

Page 92—1983 Tammy Palmer Modeling New Cap. Beth-El School of Nursing catalog cover, 1984–1985. Beth-El Alumni Collection, UCCS Archives.

Page 92—2004 Evolution of the Beth-El Uniforms. Courtesy of Jo Ruth, Beth-El Alumni Collection, UCCS Archives.

Page 93—A Diverse Institution, Beth-El College of Nursing catalog, 1984-1985, 2. Beth-El Alumni Collection, UCCS Archives.

Narrative Images References (continued)

Page 95—Beth-El General Hospital 1933 Commemorative Pen and Ink Drawing, Lydia Dazey Hornbeck handmade Yearbook 1933. Beth-El Alumni Collection, UCCS Archives.

Page 97—Beth-El Hospital Plat. E. L. Mosley, City Manager, "Interim Report to Mayor and City Council," Pikes Peak Library District, Pikes Peak Library District, Colorado Springs, 1943.

Page 98—A patient in an "Iron Lung," *Colorado Springs Gazette*, February 22, 1948.

Page 100—"Memorial Annex," *Colorado Springs Gazette*, February 22, 1948.

Page 104—Memorial Hospital Entrance and West Wing. Photo by Stewarts Commercial Photographers, Grace Bodenestine Heath collection Beth-El Alumnae Scrapbooks Vol. I 38. Beth-El Alumni Collection, UCCS Archives.

Page 105—c 1955 Nursing Arts Laboratory, *Beth-El College of Nursing* catalog Vol. I 38. Beth-El Alumni Collection, UCCS Archives.

Page 116—Beth-El Historians. Photo courtesy of Jo Ruth, Beth-El Alumni Collection, UCCS Archives.

Page 125—Beth-El College of Nursing (10 N. Farragut with 7 students), Beth-El College Nursing

Catalog 1987–1988, 10.

Page 126—An Evolution of Beth-El Nursing Pins, Photo by Cheri Robinson Gillard, Beth-El Alumni Collection, UCCS Archives.

Page 137—2004 Beth-El College of Nursing and Health Sciences in University Hall, UCCS Campus, Courtesy of Joanne Ruth, Beth-El Alumni Collection, UCCS Archives.

Page 139—Students Modeling Beth-El Uniforms with Jo Ruth, 2004 Courtesy of John Rowland., Beth-El Alumni Collection, UCCS Archives.

Page 147—Sunshine and Happy Children on the Children's Pavilion Porch. 1914, courtesy Margaretta M. Boas collection, Pikes Peak Library District.

Page 148—Six Children on Wooden Glider Swing. Julia Ray Work collection. Beth-El Alumni Collection, UCCS Archives.

INDEX

Made in the USA
Charleston, SC
27 April 2016